# Sow It
• 
# Grow It
•
# Know It

*In a North Alabama Garden*

## Mary Lou McNabb

*This book is dedicated to all
Master Gardeners in
Alabama —
in appreciation of your
volunteer hours to help
make our state a better
place to live.*

Copyright © 2017 by Mary Lou McNabb

All rights reserved. No portion of this book may be reproduced — mechanically, electronically, or by any other means, including photocopying, without written permission of the author.

Cover Photograph by Robert McNabb
Edited by Andria Cummings
Designed by Cathy Gamble
Photography by Robert McNabb, unless otherwise credited.
Line drawings by Mary Lou McNabb, unless otherwise credited.

Alabama Master Gardeners logo used with permission by the Alabama Master Gardeners Association, Inc.

Scroll artwork on title pages and color insert by kotoffei/IStock/Thinkstock
Color insert illustrations:
Lavender, parsley, oregano and thyme by ElenaMedvedeva/IStock/Thinkstock
Blueberries by elyaka/IStock/Thinkstock
Chrysanthemum and rose by 7romawka7/IStockThinkstock
Grapevine by WaffOzzy/IStock/Thinkstock

Printed by Tennessee Valley Press, Inc., Decatur, AL
USA

ISBN 978-0-692-85902-5

# Table of Contents

Mary Lou McNabb Award ........................................................................ 4

Introduction ............................................................................................. 5

Chapter 1: Blueberry Cultivation ............................................................. 9

Chapter 2: Small Fruits .......................................................................... 25

Chapter 3: A Year in the Herb Garden ................................................... 33

Chapter 4: Beneficial Bugs, Birds, Bats and Biochar ............................. 61

Chapter 5: Gremlins in the Garden (Pests) ............................................ 71

Chapter 6: Variety of Vegetables ............................................................ 99

Chapter 7: Lots of Lists ........................................................................ 125

Chapter 8: Connoisseur's Collection of Cultivars ................................ 131

Chapter 9: Heard in the Blueberry Patch ............................................ 143
*True Tales to Tickle and Tantalize You.*

Chapter 10: Month-By-Month in the Garden ..................................... 161

*1997 Mary Lou McNabb Award presented to Mary Lou McNabb (L) by Dot Saunders (R) at 1997 Alabama MG Conference, Gadsden, Alabama*

## Mary Lou McNabb Award Presented

Mary Lou McNabb was selected to receive the very first Mary Lou McNabb Award for 1997, as outstanding Alabama Master Gardener Volunteer of the Year.

Each year, as new Master Gardener Volunteers of the Year are selected, their names will be added to the Mary Lou McNabb Award Plaque which has proudly been placed at the State Extension Headquarters at Auburn University.

*Photo and information reprinted with permission from "The Alabama Master Gardener Newsletter," May 1997*

# Introduction

I have written this book to help others appreciate the beauty of the Earth and all of its amazing creatures and to encourage all who read it to preserve it for generations to come.

This is my own story of wanting to live in the country: I loved flowers even when a child and spent many summers with my sister, brother and mother on my grandparent's farm in north Louisiana. There were always farm animals, cow, pigs, mules, and dogs, cats and chickens for pets, and often a goat, which would be sold after we left and Dad took us back to West Texas in the fall. My grandmother also loved flowers and sold daffodil bulbs, eggs, figs and pears as a supplement to the farm income.

During my husband's engineering career, we moved many times and always lived in cities, but I never forgot those childhood days. Fortunately, my children all experienced this same farm life for a few days for several summers. As the children grew up, we had a dog most of those years and dogs require exercise to be lovable pets. A farm is the perfect place for that.

I grew flowers everywhere we lived and learned about different climates and the plants that thrived in each one. I had a few small vegetable plots over the years, but after our youngest child left for college, we were finally able to move to a farm. At last, I had space to grow a multitude of flowers, herbs and vegetables.

Flowers were important for esthetic beauty and for using in floral designs that were necessary for becoming a flower show judge. Of course, flowers are easily accessible, but the ones I grew myself produced plant materials that were not commercially available for flower arranging.

I enjoyed learning about herbs and their culinary use as I prepared meals. Vegetables are easily purchased in the grocery store or farmers markets, and there is a great trend to supply organically grown ones. I want to know the history of the food I am going to eat. Many exceptionally flavorful cultivars are not available in the market, and most tomatoes, cucumbers and other produce is coated with food-quality paraffin to keep it from deteriorating while being shipped long distances. Gardening is good exercise and I enjoy observing nature. Meal planning is easy and convenient if there are vegetables and herbs nearby. Last of all, but maybe most important, it is thrifty.

## What is Your Climate?

We live in zone 7a as designated by the U.S. Department of Agriculture's Plant Hardiness Zone Map. If you live elsewhere, you can find your zone online at http://planthardiness.ars.usda.gov/.

I garden in a little valley between two hills about 400 feet high just on the outskirts of Huntsville, Alabama. The valley is about 600 feet wide, so it is protected somewhat from long hot days with shade part of each day in summer. There is no cement paving nearby, and we are slightly cooler than the city. A creek is located across the road at a lower elevation, the frost pocket, and our uphill side is a gradual slope facing southwest. There are extensive woodlands behind our house which is 400 feet from the road. Our gardens are downhill from the house and 200 feet from the woods. There are plenty of wild plants for the deer and other animals, but when drought comes and food is getting scarce, they begin to raid our cultivated plants.

Deer have also learned that the plants we are growing have better flavor than wild ones.

Of course, deer love azaleas but not rhododendrons. They eat camellias — just their cup of tea. After all, tea leaves are gathered from a relative of the camellia. Magnolias seem safe from deer and grow well in shade but do not bloom there. Deer also gobble up other shrubs that we would like to grow in deciduous shade such as viburnum and oak leaf hydrangea. They much prefer our cultivated hydrangeas over the wild ones. Shrubs that seem safe from deer include aucuba, crape myrtle, nandina, elaeagnus and mahonia. These last three that are deer proof are on the invasive list and will spread and take habitat from native plants.

Ornamental plants that grow in half shade or full sun, and are drought proof once established, are holly, forsythia, Japanese Andromeda (pieris), mountain laurel, spirea, Florida anise (the source of star anise pods that are used as herbs,) Cornelian Cherry, dogwood, boxwood and pearl bush (exochorda racemosa). I emphasize drought proof because these plants are never given supplemental water.

How does your garden situation compare to mine? I hope the information provided in this book will help you to be a better gardener and enjoy the bounty of whatever you grow.

— *Mary Lou McNabb, 2017*

# Origin of the Master Gardener Program in Alabama

I had just returned to live in Alabama in the Fall of 1980 when I learned that a botanical garden was being planned for Huntsville. The Master Gardener program in Binghamton, N.Y., where I had taken the course and become a Master Gardener, had established and provided support for a small botanical garden in that city. I could see that trained gardeners would be needed to support this same type of project in Huntsville. I visited my local county agent, Garey Murray, and told him he would have no peace from me until the Master Gardener Program became a reality in Huntsville.

Two professors from Alabama A&M, Dr. Caula Beyl and Dr. Govind Sharma, collaborated with Garey Murray and me to plan a program based on materials I had received from the extension service in New York state. Bulletins from Southern states were substituted and similar topics would be taught. Alabama A&M and the Bennett Nursery of Huntsville were very supportive in organizing the program. I was very pleased that the program was implemented in the Spring of 1981 in Huntsville. Thirty Master Gardeners were trained in the first class. Much of our volunteer work was performed at the A&M campus and subsequently, at the new botanical garden site. It has been a rewarding experience and I am extremely pleased that the Master Gardener program has been enthusiastically embraced throughout Alabama.

— *Mary Lou McNabb, 2017*

*Alabama Master Gardeners logo used with permission by the Alabama Master Gardeners Association, Inc.*

CHAPTER • ONE

# Blueberry Cultivation

We began the blueberry planting in 1982 with 400 bushes. Early in 1986, Auburn University asked us to evaluate four new varieties of blackberries for production in north Alabama. At this time, there were very few thornless blackberry varieties, so the plants that were chosen had thorns. Auburn would furnish the plants and get them planted and we would record the poundage of each cultivar for several years. The end result was to determine what varieties were best for this area.

We prepared two rows for the plants. A professor from Auburn and our Madison County Extension agent did the planting in May of 1986. Four-inch long roots were planted horizontally 3 inches deep and spaced 16 inches apart in the row. Cultivars were chosen at random so no one cultivar would receive the best or worst location. Drip irrigation, trellises and signs were installed. Customers would be required to pick each variety in a separate bucket to determine the harvest. That first summer, roots were getting established and leaf stalks grew 28 inches tall before winter arrived. In the spring of 1987, the plants grew very well and began to bear fruit.

Blackberry plants bear on the growth of the previous year that is called floricanes or "flowering canes." Our blueberry bushes were just beginning to bear fruit and we were ready to begin selling blueberries to pick-your-own customers from Huntsville and the surrounding area.

## What Shall I Wear to Go Pick Blueberries?

If you are an avid gardener, you know it is going to be hot out there when summer comes. Have you thought about what to wear to be the most comfortable in the garden? Many people who came to pick blueberries when we had the business of pick-your-own didn't last long even if they arrived at 7:00 a.m. or 8:00 a.m. on a summer day. They were wearing black polyester T-shirts and black shorts. They were dressed to sweat! You will be wise to forget fashion and try for comfort. My sister always declared that if you are comfortable, you surely aren't stylish!

Wear light colors (other than yellow that attracts insects) and clothing made of cotton. It is hard to find clothing of all cotton fabric, and I make most of my gardening clothes during the winter. (It is even hard to find all cotton fabric for sale!) I always wear a hat, but not sunglasses, for picking berries. Why not sunglasses? Customers came to the sales barn after picking a bucket of blueberries and took off their sunglasses only to find they had picked many unripe berries. They had to buy them because they had chosen them. Blueberries will turn blue after being picked, but they do not sweeten once harvested. This is true of strawberries and blackberries, also. You see the birds out in the field eating berries before they are ripe, but birds will eat almost anything.

---

### Bumper Stickers

One Saturday morning a shiny new sports car came speeding up the driveway. The man at the wheel was dressed in the latest fashion of dark shorts and T-shirt. He pulled up in the parking area and slammed on the brakes in a cloud of dust. There were railroad ties placed at the front of the parking area and, unknown to him, the front bumper of his car extended over the railroad tie. The family got out, mama, dad and two pre-teen kids, and went to the field to pick berries. They were all dressed in "stylish" black, probably knitted of polyester. They soon had a few berries and came to the barn and paid for their berries. They all got in that shiny new sports car and with a swift move in reverse and then forward, they roared down the driveway feeling very proud of themselves.

Later that morning, I noticed something shiny lying in the parking area. Sure enough, the bumper from that shiny new sports car had caught on the railroad tie, and when the car left, the bumper stayed behind! I'm sure the owner wondered what happened to the car bumper, but he never came back to retrieve it. We put it out at the curb after a few days, and someone decided to take it. Recycling at its best! Sorry the bumper was lost, but glad the railroad tie remained intact.

We advertised blackberries and blueberries in the local paper and put up our MARYMAC FARM sign. A few people came and wanted to pick blackberries. Everyone knew how good blackberries were in jam, pies and other desserts. We let them pick blackberries and then asked them to try the blueberries. No one seemed to know what to do with blueberries or how to pick them. Well, at least there were no thorns. We printed a few recipes using blueberries and gave them to our pickers, and they gradually developed a taste for blueberries.

We continued the blackberry production for many years. After four years, I was invited to give a lecture about the blackberry experiment to the Alabama Fruit and Vegetable Growers Association. Several color slides and charts were prepared, and the lecture was well received. This was the first time a woman had given a lecture. The male members were courteous but a little surprised that a woman could farm. Several years went by before we had a steady flow of customers to pick blueberries, but eventually their health benefits were discovered and our business thrived. We still have a few blackberry plants, but mainly for our own use.

> Before blueberry season had arrived, a visitor who had come to see flowers, asked, "What are those bushes with the green balls on them?" Blueberries were a new crop in those days.

## Blueberry Planting

There are several things to consider before you plant a blueberry bush. They need acid soil with a pH of 4 to 5.5 and a sunny location. Next to your house may not be the best choice. The foundation contains cement that will leach alkaline residue. During excavation for the foundation, the soil becomes compacted and will not drain well. If on the west side, the sun will be extremely hot. This is detrimental to the root system. The rabbit eye cultivars grow 15 feet tall and 6 feet wide. Do you have space for such a large plant? Bees will be abundant during flower production and may be a hazard to humans passing by.

The best advice is to plant them as a background part of your backyard and enjoy their color variations as the seasons change. Spring brings many small white urn-shaped blooms that hang downward and the bees will pollinate them for the subsequent berry crop. The branches that are bearing fruit in the current season will bear fruit for several years, but new tender shoots that come after harvest will bear the largest berries in two years. In December, the leaves turn red before being shed — a special treat for the eyes. As the bushes age, the mature branches have exfoliating bark.

If you have purchased a plant in a two-gallon nursery can, it is probably two feet tall and three years old. If it is spring, it may be blooming. This plant has been in a container all of its life and the roots are most likely crowded and circling the inside of the can. You will need to tease roots on the outside of the root ball loose so they will grow in the surrounding soil. As with bare root plants, do not set any deeper than they grew in the nursery pot. No fertilizer is used at planting. After planting and watering, apply a mulch of pine straw or other organic material. It will moderate the soil temperature in all seasons and retain moisture for the root system. The blooms should be removed in the first season to get the root system well established. Weeds and grass compete with your plant for nutrition and water and should be eliminated as much as possible until the plants have become established.

---

•

Rabbit eye blueberries are of the family vaccinium ashei. We use the rabbit eye cultivars here because they thrive in well-drained clay soil that is amended with humus. Their close relative, the highbush blueberry, requires colder temperature than we have in north Alabama. It also prefers sandy soil, so it needs humus added to aid in retaining moisture. The fruits are slightly larger but do not keep as well as the rabbit eye berries.

•

---

## Commercial Planting of Blueberries

The recommended spacing for rabbit eye blueberry orchards is 6 feet apart in the row and rows 12 feet apart. Mail order plants are usually received bare root between late November and late February. Plants purchased in containers may be planted at any season. Holes are prepared in advance. Do not dig holes with a spade as this will leave smooth sides that the roots may not be able to penetrate.

Many plants have died because the clay sides of the planting hole were impenetrable. Work one generous shovel of humus into each hole. This may be Canadian sphagnum peat moss, leaf mold or acid compost. Any rocks more than one inch in diameter should be removed and the humus well mixed with the soil in the planting hole. Bushes must not be set any deeper than they were growing at the nursery. This easily can be determined by the traces of soil remaining on a bare root plant. If using bare root plants, roots should be spread out on a cone of soil in the planting hole before it is refilled. If rain is not imminent, plants benefit from a generous watering. Blueberry plants have shallow feeder roots and these must be kept continually moist for the plant to grow well. Most plants have tiny root hairs, but blueberries do not have these, making it more important to apply water if rain does not occur. In the first growing season, the blooms are removed to aid in root development. In late March, a tablespoon of fertilizer for azaleas and other acid-loving plants may be applied. As the plants grow, larger amounts of fertilizer may be applied.

Spread the fertilizer in a circle at the edge of the branch area, which will be where feeder roots are present. This is repeated in mid-August to stimulate the fall spurt of growth. The plants need nitrogen most when they are young. Ammonium sulfate is pure nitrogen and consists of white granules. Always wear gloves when working with it or your hands may get burned if they are the least bit sweaty. If granules fall on the lower leaves, shake the bush and make it fall off or the leaves will be damaged. Ammonium sulfate is an oxidizer-type of fertilizer and must be applied just before a rain or watered in after application. If this is not done, it will oxidize and not be of any benefit to the plant. Store extra ammonium sulfate in a cool dry location. Never use manure on blueberries.

> If you have only a few plants, a fertilizer for azaleas and other acid-loving plants can be bought in four-pound bags.

Blueberries have few insect or disease problems and, once established in acid soil and given plenty of water, are vigorous plants. Our field is on a slight slope and faces southwest. The slope provides good drainage, and we have a drip irrigation system to keep the soil moist in periods of drought. Occasionally, the leaves on 'Tifblue' plants become chlorotic.

(Green veins but yellow leaf area around the veins.) This is an indication that the soil may not be acidic enough for the plants to take up iron as needed. If this happens to your plant, have your soil tested and add sulfur as recommended. Application of Ironite granules will be of some help if watered in. Over several weeks, the yellow should disappear and new green leaves return.

In an extremely wet year, many berries that are ripe split open and are lost. Others have been lost before growing large enough to ripen because of mummy berry disease. The bushes had not been thinned and the thick foliage provided the right conditions for this disease to occur. Blooms had been pollinated, but the immature berries dried up and dropped off of the plants. This is a serious disease and much pruning and additional mulch of the soil to cover the diseased berries will have to be done to prevent it from recurring. Commercial fields that are not mulched have been plowed up to get rid of this disease. Sometimes older branches die to the ground and we just cut them off at soil level. There are several root rot organisms and perhaps an insect that cause this condition. When ripe berries split, bees, wasps and other insects, including Japanese beetles, soon discover them and attack the split berries. On rare occasions there has been an invasion of fruit worms, but these were not serious. We have never used insecticides in our field because of consideration for our bees. Our beekeeper was happy about that, and we sold honey for him for many years.

Honey bees are great pollinators, and wild bees and bumble bees also pollinate the blooms. If you watch a bumble bee at work on a bush, you will see it split the side of the bloom to get the nectar as the bumble bee is too large to get inside the bloom. The resulting berry may have a slight mark on one side, but it is not damaging.

After harvest, fertilizer is applied. Pruning must be done before the end of September when a spurt of growth will occur before dormancy sets in. This tender growth must mature enough to survive the coming winter, and if rain does not fall, watering must be done. In late November when we have had some freezing weather, the leaves turn a bright red before being shed in late December. We never attempt to rake them, but just leave them to decompose under the bushes. We try to keep mulch three or four inches deep under each bush using partly decayed leaf mold, or pine straw, if it is free of weed seeds.

After the first year, the amount of fertilizer is gradually increased until at two years it will be two tablespoons twice a year. At five years of age, one-half cup of fertilizer, twice a year, is a reasonable feeding. This is probably the maximum amount to apply even when the bush reaches the mature age of 15 years. Late March and again in late August are the preferred times to fertilize and hope for rain or do some watering to get the fertilizer working.

By using decayed leaf mold as mulch, we have not used any chemical fertilizer for many years. If good care is provided, including pruning, mulching and watering, bushes may live and produce more than 40 years. When they are five years old, the bark begins to exfoliate. The scaly growth will be shed. Do not be concerned, as this is normal. When the branches get many years old, the bark will be rough and that is an indication that these branches need to be removed.

## Pruning Advice

If pruning is not done in August, it would be better to wait until late March to prune. This is very hard for the gardener to do because it means reducing the oncoming crop. Therefore, August, even though the weather is hot and humid, is the preferred time to prune. (Dead twigs and branches may be removed at any season.)

Good tools needed for pruning are a hand pruner, either of anvil or bypass type, and a folding type pruning saw with a six-inch blade. A replacement blade should be on hand. We have also used a reciprocating saw that is battery-powered, but the cut is not as neat. An extra battery is always in the charger, and even though this blade is only three inches long, it is harder to get to the base of most old branches at soil level. Bypass pruners give a clean cut, but anvil may be easier to use in some situations. Always make a clean cut and do not leave ragged edges on the plant.

Just as important, do not leave stubs above a node. If you do, these stubs will die back and invite rot or disease. In the months to come, if you pruned out large old stems at the soil level, you will observe many small sprouts coming below your cut. These need to be thinned out or your bush will be too crowded with center growth. The berries will be hard to pick and not be as large as if you had thinned out the inside branches. Always favor the outward growth. The supplementary pruning to be done will be removing low growing branches that would fall to the ground when laden with berries and removing the small twigs that grow on the inside of the bush. This is a time-consuming job, but provides larger berries and easier picking. The saying is "make the bush so open a robin could fly through it." Our motto has been: "If in doubt, take it out!"

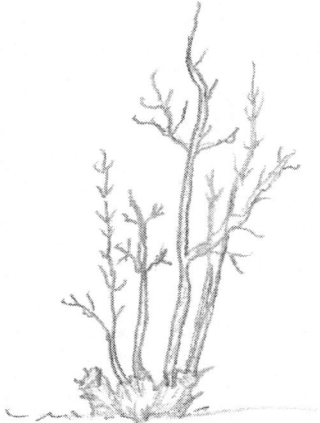

More upright growth is achieved when branches are cut 2 inches above soil.

Long drooping branches occur when cuts are made 2 feet above soil.

Each cultivar is different and each plant of the same cultivar will display an individual pattern of growth. There has not been written a standard method of pruning that will apply to all cultivars. Commercial growers just bush hog the tops of some of their acres at two feet above soil level and wait a minimum of two years for the next harvest on that group of plants. Plants start producing fruit on the second year's growth. Sometimes it may take a third year, depending on the weather and fertility of the soil. Of course, they have hundreds of acres of blueberries and all the work, including picking and packing, is done by machine. They will be able to "furlough" a given field for a few years.

In our field of 1,200 bushes, we have grown only five cultivars. They are all rabbit eye types. The 'Tifblue,' 'Climax,' 'Brightwell,' 'Premier,' and 'Yadkin' cultivars have been very productive. One year, our pick-your-own public gathered about 18,000 pounds. Average production was 12,000 pounds in a season of six or eight weeks. We also have one 'Baldwin' bush. It blooms very late and the berries ripen in late August and September. The birds know just where it grows!

New cultivars are introduced very often by University of Arkansas, University of North Carolina, and University of Georgia. This university in Athens, Georgia, has a website (extension.uga.edu) listing many cultivars with their growing and bearing information and you will find much good information there. We highly recommend that you try some of the newer ones, as they are bred to have larger berries. One of the recent introductions is named 'Titan' and it shows promise for the southeast.

> The rabbit eye blueberry was developed by Abraham Baldwin Agricultural Experiment Station in Tifton, Georgia. It is said that two fishermen found some plants out in the woods growing on the edge of a creek and brought them to the experiment station about 1944. They gave them to Dr. Tom Brightwell and Dr. Arlen Draper and told them the berries were good, although small. These two professors started breeding improved cultivars from this beginning and to those professors we owe our modern southern blueberry.

Many berries in the grocery store are raised in north Florida (very early bearing) and late in the season, berries are brought from Michigan. In mid-winter, they are brought from South America. Blueberries are so easily picked and frozen that you should get local berries. Because of our age and declining health, we closed our business in fall 2015. We enclose a few of our favorite recipes at the end of this chapter.

## Pruning Blueberries in Your Yard

'Tifblue' was introduced many years ago but is still one of the most successful cultivars for north Alabama. The only negative thing about this cultivar is the tendency of berries to split during periods of wet weather. If your bush is vigorous (as 'Tifblue' usually is) and five or six years old, it is time for some pruning.

We assume you have done minor pruning in previous years to remove crossing branches and low twiggy branches which only bear small berries and hinder weed control. A vigorous 'Tifblue' bush will have many new sprouts emerging over an area of one square yard. If these have not been trampled down by foot traffic, they may have become several feet tall. Some will have grown roots in the soil area if covered with mulch and given plenty of water.

Rooted suckers can be cut off near the base of the parent plant and transplanted or potted during the dormant season. Most will not be branched and, after replanting or potting, cut the top growth back by half. On most plants, other than blueberries, tip pinching will cause latent buds to emerge on the stem below. However, I have found that removing only a short tip on a blueberry bush will produce a second tip that will continue to grow tall. If you do any tip pinching, remove at least six inches of the tip to stimulate side growth.

When older growth is removed by sawing it off at soil level, or as near soil level as possible, many new sprouts will arise and these are thinned out by rubbing them off while they are less than two inches tall. This will thin out the subsequent growth and pay off in the long term. By November and December, the more mature branches, one year old and older, will have tiny dark brown pointed tips in the leaf axil about one-sixteenth of an inch long. These are fruiting buds for next summer's berries.

As the summer growing season takes place, many vigorous shoots will have grown six feet tall or perhaps even taller. We used to cut these one-inch-in-diameter canes back at two feet above soil level. In later years, they bore good berries, but the branches were heavy with fruit and fell down between the rows. It was hard to get the mower between the rows. Resulting berries were dusty from the mower or so close to the soil that they were hard to harvest. We decided this was a mistake, and later began to cut them off at soil level or let a tall person pick those berries. This has proved to be a better method of pruning.

When we had 1,200 bushes, our method of pruning required two people working together. One person with a saw and loppers worked underneath the bush, and the other person chose the trunks to be removed, pulling the trunks slightly at an angle so the saw did not bind, and pulling out the trunks as they were cut. This "above person" usually made the major decisions and also did the "finish" work after the major cuts were made. When these major trunks were removed, it was easier to find and remove the smaller unwanted growth. As before, our motto was "If in doubt, take it out!" This is only a good motto if the bush is growing vigorously.

## Climax Pruning

Climax bushes have a different growth pattern and therefore, the pruning practice is different. They are not as vigorous and rapid growing as 'Tifblue,' and require less pruning. They emerge from a central area but may have several large trunks if they are over six years old and have grown well.

The oldest trunks are sawed off close to the soil level. They can be identified by their size (older is larger) and will have a grained bark. They may be covered with lichen if air circulation has been poor. After one-quarter to one-third of the major trunks are removed, there will be six to eight trunks remaining. New growth will emerge from the central area, but Climax is less vigorous than other cultivars so we do not rub off any new sprouts on the stump.

> Climax blueberry bushes will make excellent bonsai specimens because, after straight growing branches have borne berries and are pruned, vigorous new growth from the main branch frequently appears at a 90-degree angle. This type of growth is the key to good Bonsai design.

This is my favorite cultivar for eating fresh, probably because it is the first to have ripe berries. The first berry to ripen is called the "king berry." In most fruiting plants, it is the largest of a cluster. (Remember those extra-large strawberries you had at the first of the season?)

Our other cultivars are pruned by these same methods depending on the type of growth each presents. Look at that just pruned bush and ask yourself "can a robin fly through it?" (Now you understand why no reliable work has been published on "How to prune a blueberry bush.")

When the pruning is finished, all trimmings are removed from the field and burned. This keeps the field neat and permits mowing of the grass strips between rows. For cross pollination, we planted two long rows of one cultivar and then next to that, two long rows of a different cultivar. They may not bloom at exactly the same time, but cross pollination does occur and there are heavy loads of berries on each stem. You need at least two different cultivars for good pollination and fruit set.

Weed control has been a constant problem. If you have a good stand of nearly weed free lawn or pasture before you begin, it is a great advantage. You must be careful when using any herbicide to avoid hitting young sprouts. They are easily damaged. We have used only Round Up (glyphosate) and I have occasionally hit a new sprout. If I did not cut it off immediately, it kept growing but had deformed leaves and had to be removed eventually. Even hoeing the area under a bush must be done carefully to avoid damaging shallow roots. The best weed control is the hardest — just get down there and pull those weeds and promise yourself that you will apply more mulch!

## Propagation by Cuttings

Blueberries are propagated from semi-mature wood in late May or early June. Make cuttings from shoots near the base of the plant that are pencil thick. One stem may make several cuttings of six or eight inches in length. Strip off lower leaves and insert in a well-drained medium. Press medium firmly around it with three inches below the surface. If you do not have a mist system, use rooting hormone. Misting will be needed if you cannot supply a closed container for the cuttings. Under a mist system, cuttings will root in six or eight weeks unless there is extreme heat or the mist has failed. When roots are two inches long, pot in individual four-inch pots and place in shade. It will be hot at this time. Keep moist and in shade until fall frost threatens. A cold frame is needed to avoid frozen roots. Do not allow the roots to freeze or plants will die. In late spring, if they are showing new growth, they may be planted in a "nursery" bed to be tended carefully while growing larger, or moved up to gallon pots. When they are two feet tall, plant them in the garden or field, water well and apply two or three inches of mulch. Be aware that moles and other underground creatures are going to try to tunnel in this newly planted area. Continue to push soil down where there are tunnels. All blooms should be removed for two years. In three or four years, these young plants will begin producing a good crop.

Now that you are growing some blueberry bushes, you need to know how to pick and freeze those berries. It is important to know not to pull the berries from the bush. When ripe, they will easily fall into your palm with just a little twist. After picking, they will turn blue, but not become sweeter, so taste the berries before you gather a large amount. Commercial berries are picked by machines that straddle the row, have a catch basin below the bush and a shaker that dislodges the berries that are ripe.

We cringe when we see a customer bring a five-gallon bucket in which to pick. Have some pity on those berries in the bottom of the bucket — you will crush them under their own weight! We use only one-gallon buckets. A gallon weighs just a little over 5 1/2 pounds.

After picking, bring them into your kitchen. Do not wash them. The "bloom" that is the slight coating on the berries protects them from drying out.

Pour your berries in a single layer on trays lined with paper towels and let them come to room temperature and allow all moisture to evaporate. Sort and remove stems and trash before placing them in freezer bags in your freezer. Dry berries will not stick together and when you want to use them, just pour out as many as you need and enjoy. We never wash our berries because they are washed by the rain and have never been sprayed with chemicals. If you must wash your berries, do so just before serving. If they are still frozen, you will have ice crystals form on them.

> •
> Commercial growers sometimes spray a bird repellent called Thiram on their bushes and the berries must be washed to remove this before packaging. Thiram causes the birds to choke up as they eat, and they are less likely to raid a field.
> •

## Bird-proof Your Bushes

Our customers often ask us what we do about the birds. We tell the customers that they are our live scarecrows and we are glad they came! Of course, the birds really enjoy those berries and get their fill of them when the customers are gone. With only a few bushes, you will have to fight off the birds. Birds do not wait until the berries are ripe before starting to eat them.

A mesh net with one-half-inch openings can be used to cover the bushes, but mockingbirds are very clever and will find any openings that exist and get inside to eat berries. If you can build a structure over your bushes and cover it with the net, it will be more effective. Make the structure taller than the bushes to allow for growth and avoid birds landing on the net and pecking berries through the openings. It must be fastened down at the soil level to really make it bird proof.

## Basic Considerations When Planting a Blueberry Bush:

- You must provide acid soil with a pH of 4 to 5.5.
- When pruning, always favor new growth and let it remain.
- Remove twiggy growth — only small berries will result.
- "Lift the skirt" — remove low branches.
- Cut back new canes at least four to six inches or just a new tip will form.
- Don't trim side shoots just a little — the bush will be too thick and berries hard to find.
- Cut young vigorous canes only in the center of the bush to 2 1/2 feet, so new growth will be low enough to reach for picking.
- Cut outside canes at soil level and if numerous new sprouts occur, rub off many of them.
- In winter, only prune off dead growth.
- Prune in August or March.
- Fertilize right after pruning is finished, using a formula for acid loving plants.
- Keep weeds and tree seedlings removed.
- Water. Mulch. Pray for no late frosts!

# Recipes

In the following recipes, you may use equal amounts of blueberries and blackberries, or blueberries and sliced peaches. When using frozen berries, allow them to thaw before making these recipes.

## Blueberry Mystery Cake *Recipe*

**Bottom layer:**
Spread in greased 8x8 Pyrex dish, 2 cups blueberries. Sprinkle with 1 tablespoon of lemon juice.

**Topping:**
1/2 cup sugar
1 tablespoon cornstarch
Mix together until no lumps are present and set aside.

**Cake batter:** Cream together:
3 tablespoons butter/margarine
3/4 cup sugar

Sift together:
1 cup flour
1 teaspoon baking powder
1/8 teaspoon salt

Measure 1/2 cup milk and set aside.

Add sifted dry ingredients to creamed sugar and butter alternately with milk. Pour this batter over berries in baking dish. Sprinkle cornstarch and sugar topping evenly over batter. Heat 1 cup water to boiling and pour gently over batter. Do not stir.

Bake at 400 degrees about 40 minutes. Serve warm.

## Blueberry Crunch Cake *Recipe*

1 20-ounce can crushed pineapple with juice

3 cups blueberries

1/2 cup sugar

1 box yellow cake mix (Duncan Hines with pudding added is great)

1 1/2 sticks butter, melted

1 cup chopped pecans

Pour pineapple with juice into 9x13 baking pan and spread evenly. Sprinkle blueberries over pineapple. Sprinkle sugar over blueberries. Spread dry cake mix over sugar. Pour melted butter evenly over cake mix.

Sprinkle chopped pecans on top.

Bake at 350 degrees for 35 to 45 minutes until lightly brown.

*You will note that there is no mixing and the only dish to be washed is a measuring cup in which you melted the butter.*

## Quick and Easy Blueberry Cobbler

*Recipe*

I have used half blueberries and half blackberries or half blueberries and a sliced peach when making cobblers. These combinations are very tasty. Using your microwave really saves time and eliminates several clean up chores. I have written this recipe so that an inexperienced cook can understand each process.

I always place a sheet of aluminum foil underneath this cobbler as it may run over. Preheat oven to 400 degrees.

Place in 8-inch-square Pyrex dish that is two inches deep: 2 or 3 cups blueberries and two tablespoons of liquid. (Water or fruit juice from canned fruit may be used). Cover with plastic wrap and place in microwave oven. Cook on high for 2 minutes.

While this is cooking, mix together 2 tablespoons corn starch and ½ cup sugar.

Remove dish from oven. Be careful, it is hot. Discard plastic wrap. Sprinkle cornstarch/sugar over berries and stir gently to mix. (If berries were very sweet, add 1 teaspoon of lemon juice. Bottled is fine). Return cobbler to microwave and cook for additional 2 minutes on high.

While this is cooking, put 1 1/4 cups biscuit mix in bowl and add 1/2 cup milk. Stir to make a soft dough. You may need to add another tablespoon of milk if this dough is too thick to drop.

Remove baking dish from microwave and drop spoons full of dough over the hot berries. Put in standard oven and bake about 20 minutes or until slightly browned.

CHAPTER • TWO
# Small Fruits

Blackberries, raspberries, strawberries and grapes are delicious and have their own distinct flavor. Each also has its own characteristics that must be considered when growing them.

## Blackberries

Blackberry plants need attention in the early part of the year. The bearing canes from last year should have been removed after the harvest was over in late July or early August. Remove them now, if not done last fall. These dead canes are in the way and the new canes will have grown up into them.

January is the time to cut back the new canes that are the long canes that grew after last season's berries were harvested. These are called floricanes. These canes should be cut off four feet above the soil line. Each time you shorten these vigorous canes, it will cause branching on the remaining part that will bear the fruit for the current season. Most blackberry plants need some support to hold them upright, and prevent the berries from getting splashed with dirt during storms. Berries are hard to clean without losing them, so training on a support really pays off.

We have driven strong stakes into the soil eight feet apart and strung wire between them four feet above the soil and trained the plants up on the wires. After pruning and until they start to grow in spring, you will need to tie them loosely where you want them to grow.

Whether to prune or not to prune is always a difficult decision. You make a few mistakes, but there is always next year. 'Triple Crown' is an excellent large fruited, thornless, and flavorful blackberry.

## Raspberries

Raspberries are much sought after, but difficult to grow in hot climates. 'Dormanred' has been the most successful in the south. We have had some luck with 'Dinkum,' which bears few berries at a time, but still has ripening fruits into late fall. There are no thornless cultivars, but raspberry thorns are not as numerous as those on thorny blackberries.

Packaged shoots are available in spring and are planted 10 inches apart in rows. Soon there will be many suckers arising from each individual plant. These can be transplanted to new locations and you soon will have a large patch. Training and pruning are identical to blackberries. These berries do not require fertile soil or excessive water after becoming well established.

Picking requires some care. Raspberries are very fragile and the fruit must be handled gently. The core of each berry remains on the stem and if the vine is shaken, ripe fruits drop off on the ground. This was the big problem with allowing customers to enter our netted row to gather the berries. They will be eaten by birds if not covered. We decided it was not worth our time and effort to try to produce raspberries and we stopped growing them. You may make that decision also after a season or two.

## Strawberries

Strawberry plants are offered for sale in spring and most are the everbearing 'Quinault' cultivar. Pick-your-own fields on the outskirts of Huntsville do not grow these because they never have an abundance of berries at one time. June-bearing plants, which produce in May in our area, have a large number of fruits over a few weeks and then the season is over for the year.

If early blooms are not killed by frost in late March, the harvest begins in early May. I faithfully covered my blooming plants with row cover or pine straw every time frost was predicted or the temperature was to be in the low thirties or lower. Row cover cannot be left over the plants as bees need to pollinate the blooms. Most berried plants produce the largest berry on the first pollinated bloom, the king berry. Harvesting of the first large king berries began in late April.

Ordering plants is the only way to get disease-free cultivars to plant. Twenty-five plants of a cultivar are in a package and are shipped in late fall or early spring. If set out in September or October, you will harvest the following May. Prepare raised rows four feet apart and set plants with the crown (the thickest part of the stem) just at soil level spaced on 18-inch centers.

> •
> There are methods of leaving the crop intact for a second year, but the runners will have become so thick that berries cannot be easily picked and there will be no place to put your feet without stepping on berries or plants. Idealists say plow out the center of the old row and leave the runners to produce the following year. It doesn't work that way in our long growing season.
> •

We have used 'Cardinal,' 'Chandler' and 'Arking' with good results. Mulch is needed to keep the berries clean. Pine straw, snuggled under the bearing stems of the mother plant, will provide clean berries but when you change the location of your patch, it must be gathered and removed to get ready for a different crop. Pine straw does not decompose readily.

In July or August, after each season of picking, we choose the first offset — the daughter plant — to transplant to a new location. Transplanting can be done as late as September. Plant scientists determined that these daughter plants, that now become the new mother plants, produce better berries in the following year than runners growing further from the original mother plant. If most of the runners that grow from the new mother plants are removed, spacing will be better and fewer, but larger berries will be produced.

Fertilizer (13-13-13) is given after the plants are established in late September and a light application or none at all in late March of the following spring. Too much nitrogen will produce lots of greenery but not many berries. Nets must be applied before the birds discover your crop. Raccoons will raid the patch at night and are clever enough to use their paws to reach through the openings in the net and get berries. Mice, moles, slugs and snails are also pests and are hard to exclude. Strawberries require "stoop labor" to harvest while blackberries and blueberries are "stand up" crops to harvest.

## Grapes

Grapes occupy a moderate amount of space in the landscape and fruit production requires a support in a sunny well-drained location. Be sure you have these requirements before planting. Muscadine grapes are descendants of the scuppernong that is native to the southeast. There are no seedless bunch grapes that are cold-hardy enough and disease-resistant to survive in our cold winters and humid summers. 'Fredonia' is a successful Concord-type bunch grape for this area.

## American Bunch Grapes

Prune grapes about the middle of January. Grapes must have severe annual pruning to bear clusters of large berries. The bunch grapes are a little more complicated to prune, but prune you must if you expect to get good production. Try to read up on the methods used or even take the picture in the book with you. If your vine is vigorous and has been in the garden for several years, when pruning, you will get rid of most of the old growth.

Choose one strong cane from last year of about pencil thickness to grow in each direction (usually medium brown in color) to bear grapes. Shorten each of these to 8 or 10 nodes. Preserve these canes and plan to fasten them to the top wire when you have finished. If there are any branches that grow vertical from the top of the main trunk, cut them

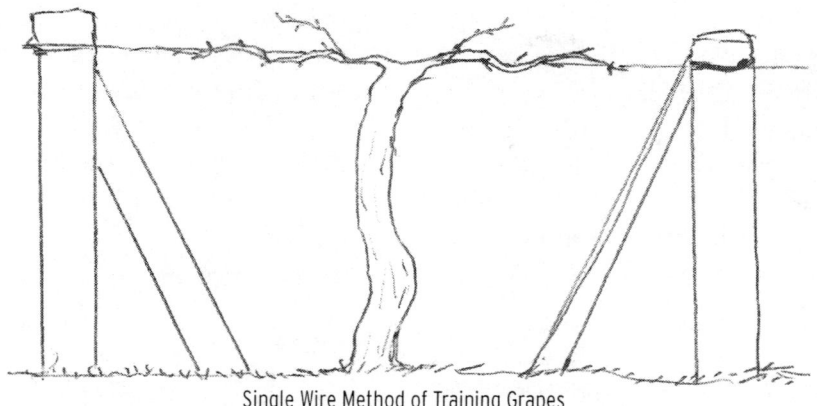
Single Wire Method of Training Grapes

off at the origin. Before you prune out all other growth, select one other cane in each direction, near the top of the vertical trunk to shorten to four nodes, to become the bearing vine in the following year.

We believe the single wire method of training is best and is shown in the illustration above. If you are using the double-wire system, choose canes in this same manner for the lower wire. Prune them as you have the top canes. There will be two canes in each direction (four canes that are long and four canes that are very short) remaining. Remove all other growth. If they have grown well in the previous year, you will have a big pile of tangled vines to discard.

Scatter a small handful of balanced fertilizer under the plant. Grapes are said to be sweeter when the vines are not given much fertilizer. When spring comes there will be new leaves and then blooms emerging from each node. If there is a hard freeze after this has occurred, do not despair. Grapes are the one plant that will send out a second set of blooms if the first ones are frost killed.

> If you want to make a grapevine wreath or basket, now is the time. Use a large bucket or tub to form a wreath while the discarded vines are fresh. Shape them around the inside or the outside of the tub or bucket, depending on what size you prefer. When the pruned off pieces have dried a few days, they will become brittle and hard to bend without breaking. They may be soaked in warm water for a few hours to become pliable again. (I don't know of anyone who has a container large enough to soak long pieces of grape prunings.)

There are some diseases that will require spraying during bloom season. If your vines receive good air circulation and there is not much humid weather or rain throughout the season, this may not be necessary. However, since we do not know what will occur, if in previous years your grapes have turned black, dried up and dropped off of the vine, it is black rot disease. When the blooms first appear (the size of a pin head) and again two weeks later, a preventive spray of fungicide will control this disease. Cleaning up the diseased fruit below the vine also will be of some help. If birds and animals raid your crop just as it is nearing ripeness in late August, you may need to place a mesh or paper bag over each cluster.

## Muscadine Grapes

Muscadine grapes are planted about 20 feet apart in the row and set deeper than when they were grown in the nursery. Keep the roots moist at all times. Only a single wire support is used and it should be about five feet above ground and supported by sturdy posts at each end of the row. Not all cultivars produce both male and female blooms. When choosing cultivars, always select at least one self-fertile type (producing both male and female blooms) for pollination of those that do not produce male blooms.

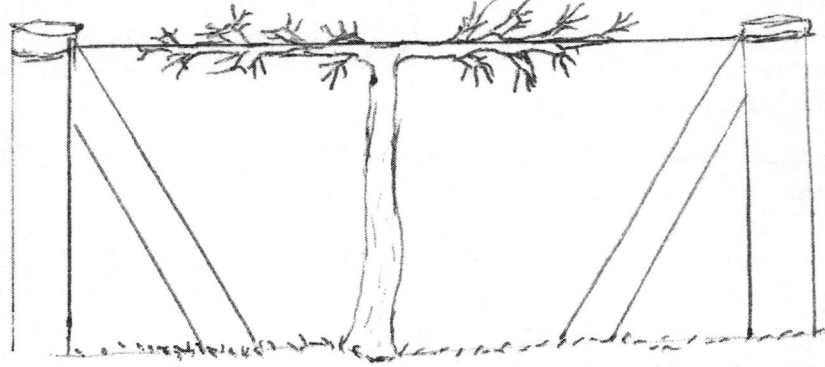

Training Muscadine Grapes

If there is only space for one vine, be sure it is self-fertile. Most all that you will find in the market place are self-fertile.

In new plantings, a slender post, that will later be removed, should be placed beside each young vine. This will give the small vine support until it reaches the five-foot wire when it will be topped to force a main arm to grow in each direction. These main arms will become large in diameter over several years and should be kept at a length of 10 feet — 20 feet for the total length of the vine. You should cut off all shoots from these main arms leaving fruiting spurs about three or four inches long. If the spurs are numerous and close together, you need to remove some so that the remaining ones are eight inches apart. There will be many buds on these shortened spurs.

> A good source of large-berried muscadine plants:
> Isons Nursery & Vineyards
> 6855 Newnan Road, PO Box 190
> Brooks, GA 30205-2424
> Phone: 800-733-0324
> Online: www.isons.com

After a few years there will be numerous long, slender pieces of vine to be cut from these spurs as you prune. If you are making a grapevine wreath, these long, slender pliable pieces are excellent to wind around the large wreath to tie it all together. The new growth on these spurs will produce leaves and buds that will be the fruit. They do not form bunches and will be picked individually from their stems. Muscadines and scuppernongs are nearly disease free.

CHAPTER • THREE
# A Year in the Herb Garden

Seasonable thoughts from the instructional poem "Five Hundred Points of Good Husbandry" by Thomas Tusser to English gardeners of 1573:

**A Little Culinary Herb Garden**
In March and in April, from morning to night,
In sowing and setting, good huswives delight:
To have in a garden, or other like plot,
To trim up their house, and to furnish their pot.
At spring (for the summer) sow garden ye shall,
At harvest (for winter) or sow not at all.
Oft digging, removing, and weeding, ye see,
Makes herb the more wholesome and greater to be.

## • JANUARY •

January is a time to reflect on your past experience of growing herbs. It is usually cold and wet at this season and not much can be done except on those occasional mild days. Do not prune anything now. Seed catalogues have arrived and there are seed racks in the stores. Wander out in your garden and pull any weeds there. Sit by the fire and think about which herbs you didn't grow that you would like to try in the coming year. Read your recipes and if you have frozen or dried some herbs, cook!

Commercial growers are starting seeds of the slow growing herbs such as sage, summer savory, marjoram and oregano. It is hard to find a good seed-propagated oregano as they are variable in growth and flavor. Divisions of a really flavorful cultivar are the best. Often those in the marketplace are oregano vulgare — the wild type. While vigorous, they are not flavorful. Before choosing oregano, pinch a leaf to smell and even put it on your tongue to test the flavor.

> Is it "herb" with the "h" pronounced or "erb" with the "h" silent? Well, when speaking of the Huntsville Herb Society, we always pronounce "h," but either is correct. The early settlers always called them "yarbs," but we knew what they meant.

Seeds of summer savory and marjoram are tiny and slow to grow but do finally make good plants if pinched frequently. Summer savory (satureja hortensis) is the annual form of this plant and winter savory, a much stronger flavor, is the perennial form. They are related, but not at all alike in appearance. Both can be grown from seeds. Summer savory has very small and tender leaves and is added to cooked foods, especially bean dishes at the end of cooking. It is easily dried and can be stored in a small jar when stripped from the stems. Do not crush until ready to use. Winter savory (satureja montana) is a robust creeping plant that produces white flowers in late summer. The leaves are sturdy and flavorful, but strong, so use small amounts and add it to the cook pot early on. Summer savory tends to reseed and you will get plants two feet tall by the end of the growing season. There will be tiny pale blue blooms that form the seeds. They are hard to separate from the stem and it is best to just rub the mature stems and save some of the resulting debris and scatter in it the planting area. Keep your seeds in a closed container in the refrigerator and they will remain viable for several years. Winter savory likes to spread over bricks or rocks and make roots there on stems that are only eight inches tall. The white

*Summer Savory*

> When sowing seeds, remember that constant moisture is necessary and even a few hours of dry soil will prevent them from germinating. Some amateur growers believe that a plastic bag or other clear cover over the flat is a good idea, but I believe it limits air circulation and causes damp off disease to develop. This is when seedlings germinate and grow well for a few days only to suddenly fall over and die. This never happens in out of doors, where there is constant air circulation.

blooms are small. They do not seem to reseed in my garden. You will need to cut the plant back in late March.

## In the Greenhouse

Rosemary cuttings may be made from greenhouse grown plants. Make cuttings five inches long, choosing the "half hard" wood. You will recognize it by the change in color of the stem. It will be pale green to almost white where the cutting should be made. Make your cut somewhere in this half hard stem just above a node and four or five inches long. Remove any buds starting to form on the cutting and also lower leaves that would be under the rooting medium. A dusting of root hormone is helpful on these winter cuttings but given warm temperature at the rooting zone, they will form roots without it. Insert two or three inches into the rooting medium and label with the date. (A vigorous cutting of rosemary will often take root in a glass of water on the window sill.) Firm the cuttings into the medium and water gently. Protect from sun for a few weeks until they are rooted and you have potted them. Once they are rooted and potted, let them get well established before pinching the tips back half an inch. This will result in a multi-stemmed plant for your garden. If you plan to make a rosemary topiary, select a young plant with a straight stem for a "lollipop" shape and use a tip-pruned plant for a miniature "tree" topiary. The "lollipop" will need the support of a sturdy stake to keep the trunk straight and strong during the development of this design. Be sure to use a stake that is 10 inches long. And as the plant grows, use twistems to attach it to the stake.

Rosemary Topiary

Pineapple sage plants over-wintered in the house or greenhouse will provide cuttings that are easily rooted in a glass of water on a warm windowsill. Try using opaque bottles in which pills are dispensed as this seems to hasten rooting. Remember to bring them away from the window at night to protect from the cold. As with all rooted cuttings, pot them when the roots are two inches long. Commercial growers root many cuttings from stock plants to produce new plants of pineapple sage to sell. Other stock plants that show signs of new growth may also be propagated from cuttings at this time. Velvet sage (salvia leucantha) roots easily but soil medium must be kept only slightly moist.

Later in the month, sow basil seeds of various kinds. They like warm temperature and will germinate quickly if it is given. Bottom heat is a great growth enhancer in the greenhouse and heat mats are available. Some of the more expensive ones have variable heat settings, but most are set at 75 degrees — the ideal temperature for most seedlings. Commercial growers sow several basil seeds in each pot and often you will find three or four young plants in pots that are for sale. It is best not to try to separate them but just set out the whole clump in your garden. After they are well established, cut off the lesser ones and allow the strongest one to grow. If you are growing your own, just sow one seed in each cell. Basil grows well once warm temperature arrives and you will be able to harvest plenty of leaves and even take cuttings from a large plant to grow more plants. A cutting of vigorous growth will root in a glass of water on the window sill in a short time.

If you do not have a greenhouse, consider setting up a florescent light garden to grow seedlings. (See January in **Chapter 10, Month By Month in the Garden**.) The important requirements are to keep the light fixture only three or four inches from the young plants and to give them a 14-hour day. A warm room and attention to moisture needs will be necessary. Watering with warm water will improve growth.

---

•

**Basil**

Some people speak in accents nasal
About their love of using basil
To confidently dramatize,
A pesto, quiche or like surprise.
Others find that they can dazzle,
Using dishes cooked with basil:
Tomato, omelet, squash or bean,
Soup or stew or aubergine.
Used in cooking, ounce by ounce,
It matters not if you pronounce
It basil ("bah")
Or basil ("bay")
You're sure to like it either way!
You'll even find this herb terrific
When called by someone scientific
Ocimum (big O) basilicum -
A lengthy name -
And rather sillicum!
Basilicum is never "bay"
It's always "bah" - no other way.
So those who use it in my castle
Say politely, "Pass the basil"!

Author unknown;
from The Herb Society of America
newsletter, 1993

•

## • FEBRUARY •

If you have potted herbs on your window sill (turn the pots around frequently to keep the growth symmetrical) or in a greenhouse, now is a good time to repot them. Choose a pot one size larger of either plastic or clay. Make your choice of the pot dependent on the eventual use of each plant. If it is to be used in a large container when spring arrives, use a plastic pot just one size larger. If it is to be kept in a pot for the next year, there will be plenty of large pots of man-made materials in the market place to choose from. (See the following section: **Growing Herbs in Containers**). Use purchased potting soil, and always moisten it before using regardless of the instructions on the bag. You may add up to one-third of the volume of perlite to potting soils to improve the drainage. When using perlite, take precautions not to inhale this dusty material. Tease roots apart as you repot and new roots will soon grow into the fresh soil.

If you used your rosemary topiary as a holiday decoration, now it can have any ornaments removed and be trimmed a little for a second year of growth. If it happened to dry out, use your finger to make some holes around the edge of the pot and pour water into them. If it does not respond to this, take it out of the pot and examine the roots. Any roots that are still white are alive and there is hope that repotting will give it new life. Alas, if all roots have turned brown, no amount of tender loving care will bring it back to life.

If you received a tree-shaped rosemary topiary as a gift, it is most likely pot bound and needs a larger pot. It was grown in a greenhouse and suffered many insults as it was transported to the store and then to the dry atmosphere of your house. Repot it also and keep pinching the new growth to preserve the tree shape. Topiary-trained plants likely will never bloom but their various shapes are the attraction. I made wire forms as a base for those that I grew and many short twistems were used to attach the branches to the frame. Planting in a clay pot and using a sturdy frame attached to the pot just under the rim provided a more secure base for the design.

This is the time to sow seeds of annual herbs such as marjoram and summer savory. These tiny seeds germinate with a very light covering of soil in a flat and grow slowly. They must have constant moisture to grow and a community flat is easier to manage. If you saved seeds of summer savory last fall, scatter them on damp potting soil and gently water. In about ten days when the first leaves appear, give them the brightest light possible whether in the window, under lights or in the greenhouse and they will become sturdy plants. Marjoram seeds are even smaller but you may be able to space them out in the flat. When they are large enough for transplanting to individual pots, this will be a great advantage.

Marjoram

## Scented Geraniums

In the greenhouse or window sill, any over-wintered plants of scented geraniums will begin to show new growth. As soon as the new growth is hardened enough to snap when bent, it is ready for making cuttings. Always choose a part of the plant that is not budded and starting to bloom, and use a single edge razor blade or knife to cut just below a node. Dip the cut stems in rooting hormone and place the leafy tops wrapped in a damp paper towel in a plastic bag. Allow the cut ends to air dry to form a callous. After the drying period of 24 hours, put the cuttings in your propagating area and press the medium firmly around them to hold them in place. If some will not stand alone, use a toothpick or chop stick to hold those upright. Keep them out of the sun for a week. During this period, you will need to mist the cuttings occasionally to avoid wilting. Keep the propagating medium only slightly moist or stem black rot may develop. After a week, expose the cuttings to more light and soon they will be able to remain turgid when exposed to full sun. Rooting usually takes several weeks. Be patient.

If you have a choice scented geranium plant and want to propagate many new ones from it, you may try a different method of rooting new plants. I have succeeded in doing this with several cultivars and discovered it quite by chance. I had a healthy mature leaf that I had removed while preparing cuttings. By chance, the leaf had a small piece of the larger stem on it at the base. I put it into a small glass of water on the kitchen window sill. It stayed there for a week or two (the water was only half inch deep) and then I decided to stick it in the cutting box. Surprise! It rooted and produced not just one plant, but several new shoots. I potted it and grew it for several weeks, before carefully separating the new shoots when they were about three inches tall and each division had a root of its own. Viola! Several plants from one leaf!

Scented Geranium propagated by new method

I am trying to improve on this chance occurrence by rooting leaves with the following method: I choose a vigorous stem with several mature leaves and cut the whole stem from the stock plant. Then, using a single edge razor blade (sterilized), I carefully cut each leaf from the stem with a small amount of the stem tissue attached. (This is called a "heel cutting" in commercial growing.) This is dipped in rooting hormone, as with the stem cuttings and then placed in the individual pot as described above. No period for a callous to form is needed. Each leaf will need to be buried half inch deep in the rooting medium to be able to stand on its own without falling over or use a toothpick to prop it up. The remainder of the conditions as stated above are used for all of the cuttings, whether stem or leaf. It usually takes a week or two longer for the leaf to get a good set of roots, but if not allowed to wilt and given good care, the result will be an increase in new plants not obtainable by using only stem cuttings. Remember that some cultivars are much easier to root than others and not all can support a new plant by using just a leaf. That leaf must have a portion of the larger stem for it to grow roots. Be sure to label with the date and cultivar for future reference. The ways to manipulate plants are very interesting and sometimes very rewarding.

## Growing Herbs in Containers

A Louisiana gardening book instructs: "Grow geraniums and pinks (Sweet William and dianthus) in large pots. In excessive water from heavy rains, drain the water off, but be faithful in watering when droughts occur. Containers may be of iron, porcelain, marble, terracotta or wooden boxes. They may be moved to protected areas during cold spells. Roses, Scented Geraniums and fragrant herbs placed near doorsteps will improve the odor of the home." The year this was written was 1838. Perhaps this advice is still relevant almost 200 years later. If you have no place in your landscaped yard or you live in an apartment, this may be a good way to grow some herbs.

You will need a location that receives at least six hours of sun each day for most herbs. The culinary herbs must be near your kitchen door for you to have access to them and containers are a good way to make this possible. If you have a deck near the door, and it has sun part of the day, you will be able to move containers around to get the most sunshine as the seasons change.

◆ **Rule 1:** *Choose a container with drainage holes in the bottom.* Usually, a piece of shard, broken clay pot scrap, is placed over the hole. You could use a few pebbles, a piece of screen wire, a scrap of old pantyhose, or something similar to cover the hole and prevent soil from washing out and insects such as sow bugs (those little many-legged creatures that roll up into a ball the size of a bb when disturbed) and snails from making a home in the bottom of the pot. Consider your style of decorating and choose a container to harmonize. If it is rustic, a half barrel would be appropriate. Other containers such as an old bushel or half bushel basket, if lined with plastic film in which holes have been punched, would be a unique planter. Look around your home and find something that can be used. Now you have found the perfect container, but it is SO deep! You can solve that problem by filling the lower section with plastic peanuts such as are used for packing fragile items. Your plants will need a minimum of eight inches of soil to grow well. After you have put in several inches of peanuts, use a piece of porous material such as pantyhose to cover the peanuts.

If your décor is formal, perhaps a concrete urn or oblong planter would be more suitable. These containers are the proper depth without adding filler. If there is no hole in the bottom, one can be drilled. Sometimes small plastic pots of plants are placed in these containers, but using the concrete container as the pot is a better plan. These heavy pots are hard to move around as the angle of the sun changes, but a strong man can do the job.

There are some large terracotta pots, usually embossed, that make attractive containers in a formal setting. They will last several years if not left out of doors in freezing weather. Terracotta pots should be soaked in water for several hours before using for the first time. Otherwise, the pot will take water away from the potting soil when watered for the first time and the plants will suffer. Clay pots dry out more readily than plastic and require water more often. Also the sun may overheat the roots inside the pot and cause them to suffer. Their greatest advantage is that they are heavy and do not turn over in wind. Many times a pot of dry soil is watered and because the soil has shrunk away from the pot sides, the water will run down the inside edge of the pot and drain out the bottom and the soil will remain dry. You can remedy this situation by punching a few holes about an inch deep in the soil with your finger and pouring the water in these holes. Pots used on a deck may be placed in a waterproof saucer to save the deck from possible deterioration.

You may want to put water in a saucer and let the soil take up the needed water in that way. This method of watering will not work if plastic peanuts have been used to fill the lower part of any pot. Heavy iron or other metal containers are sometimes available and will last for many years. These are not a good choice for summer planters as the metal absorbs heat from the sun and roots may cook. Fall and winter plantings in this type of container are successful if hardy plants are chosen.

Ah, plastic! There are many wonderful plastic or other man-made material containers available. They usually last several years and can be had for a reasonable price in any style you desire. They have one disadvantage and that is weight — or lack of it. You must have a container that will not blow over during a storm. The problem of weight can be resolved by adding some rocks in the bottom of the container. Again, place a layer of pantyhose, screen, porous fabric or landscape cloth over the rocks before adding soil. This will keep the soil from sinking down and the plants from doing the same. When choosing that plastic planter, remember that light colors are better for summer and dark colors are better for winter.

◆ **Rule 2:** *Buy good quality potting soil and moisten it before filling your container.* This can be easily accomplished by placing the soil in a large plastic bag and adding slightly warm water as you mix until the potting soil is slightly damp. When buying potting soil, it is best in the long run to choose the more expensive one. It will be weed free, have a small amount of fertilizer in it, and enough coarse material to be well drained. Most herbs are from the Mediterranean area and can be allowed to dry a bit without suffering, but you must remember that they are depending on you to water them if rains do not occur. These plants do not need excessive fertilizer, but there are a few exceptions. Parsley and mint like fertilizer and basil will do well with some extra feeding. After a month or more, your pots may need a little supplemental nutrition. When they begin to slow down, that is an indication that you need to give them a feeding of some water-soluble fertilizer such as 20-20-20. See that the soil is slightly moist and then mix the fertilizer in water in a watering can. Use only the amount recommended on the box for potted plants. More is not better. Pour the fertilizer water on the soil. In hot sun, leaves can be damaged by fertilizer on them and you will have to wash them carefully if you do not want to eat fertilizer. Keep the plants moist and, in a week or two, new leaves will appear. Now you must keep pinching and pruning to keep the new growth coming. The best time to gather your herbs is early in the morning when they are turgid and any overnight dew has dried off. Because they were grown in pots, washing may not even be required.

◆ **Rule 3:** *Larger is better.* A container with a great volume of soil is less likely to dry out if you have forgotten to water it and the rains did not come. A six- or eight-inch pot will dry out quickly on a hot day and the plant will suffer. You may use a saucer under any pot, but if there is lots of rain, the saucer will be full of water and need emptying. Remember, plants, like babies, should not sit around with wet bottoms! You can plant several compatible plants in one large container and make it attractive by using one tall plant, one spreading plant and a trailing plant. Just choose plants that like the same amount of sun and water. Rosemary and other shrub type plants are often grown as one specimen plant in a large container as they will crowd out smaller growing companions.

◆ **Rule 4:** *Choose compatible plants for combination pots.* Usually only one plant of each specie will be needed. With six hours of sun in early spring you could use cilantro, parsley and chives, as all of these are quite hardy and will not suffer in occasional light frost. As the season progresses, gather the seeds of cilantro that are now called coriander, and when the danger of frost is past, replace the cilantro with basil. Contrasting shades of green and various textures of leaves make for a more interesting combination, but choose the plants that you will use. You can have a combination pot that will serve many uses. I suggest using one parsley, one thyme and one oregano. This combination is very useful in many foods. Another pot could contain summer savory, basil and a clump of chives. These three require about the same amount of water and sun. Choose the herbs that you find most useful.

In garden centers, herb plants are available nearly all summer and the perennial ones are available even in winter. The hardier ones are such plants as rosemary, thyme, sage, and oregano. They are perennials but even these hardy plants, when grown in pots, suffer in extremely cold weather and need to be brought into a garage or other non-freezing location until warmer weather comes. They may outgrow their pots in one year and you can put them in the garden and start with young plants the following spring. If you have more shade than sun, choose mint. Always grow mint in a pot alone. It will overtake any other plant in the same pot. Unless you are renting the house, never plant mint in the garden!

◆ **Rule 5:** *Choose good plants.* Try to determine what day plants are delivered to the garden center — usually about Tuesday. When they have just arrived, they are more likely to be well watered and in prime growth. This is the time to buy! Choose young plants and let them mature in your containers. Try some new flavors in your cooking! You will discover that growing herbs in containers is fun and will not only enhance your deck or patio, but will make your food very flavorful. Perhaps foods that were not very appealing before can become a healthy mainstay in your diet when given the magic of herbs. Even if you haven't time to cook with them, they will be enjoyed just for their fragrance and ease of cultivation.

### • MARCH •

"Messy until March" has been the recommendation. Now that time has arrived, but don't be too eager to get rid of all of the dead tops. They were good protection during the winter but there will still be some cold snaps. Our usual last frost date is April 15 in zone 7a. Chive tops can be removed, as these bulbous plants are quite hardy. If you want divisions to share with a friend or tops to cut and use in your kitchen before outdoor growth begins, dig and pot up a section from a clump in your garden. Shake off as much soil as you are able. Cut back roots to about two inches. Now you will have just a section of bulbs and no tops and just some short roots. This method will get rid of most soil-borne insects. You don't want to bring them into your house or greenhouse. Use potting soil and plant the bulbs in a pot only as deep as they were in the garden. Put on a sunny cool window sill and you will soon have some to use. When harvesting chives, always cut near the soil level, as any stubs left will die.

You need to begin cutting back dead branches of winter savory and pull out any weeds that have sought shelter under their protection. If English thyme, (Thymus vulgaris) one of the taller growing cultivars used for cooking, has suffered, cut back to live growth. Creeping thyme can be divided. Use the outside vigorous sections to replant. There are many cultivars of creeping thyme and the fragrance of each is unique. One summer when I visited the Cornell University Plantations near Ithaca, New York, I saw a collection of 500 cultivars. Those with variegated leaves often lose their variegation in hot weather, but it will return when cold temperature returns. Germander, (teucrium Chamaedrys) used medicinally for centuries, can be trimmed to make an attractive hedge. A member of the mint clan, but not invasive, it has small dark green glossy leaves and grows only eight inches tall. If you want to see the pink blooms in June, let it remain untrimmed.

In the greenhouse, those seedlings of marjoram and summer savory are beginning to grow and fertilizer will help them along. They will soon be ready to put in separate pots, and pinching the tips of each stem will make them produce more leaves. Use these little snips to put on salad or add to cooked beans before serving. Set them out in the garden in late April. Keep training the topiary specimens and give them weak fertilizer monthly.

## Transplanting

When your flats of seedlings have produced their first true leaves (different from the seedling leaf), it is time to give them each a separate pot. Use deep six-packs you kept over from last year's plants that are clean and in good condition, or four-inch pots, or even deep yogurt cups that have several holes punched in the bottom. Use plenty of good quality potting soil, moistened. Find a comfortable place to work.

Place a portion of potting soil in each individual pot and press it to one side of the pot so the root of the seedling can be allowed to go deep in the pot before adding more soil. If you allow the flats to dry slightly, when you remove the whole group by turning it upside down in your hand and then turning it right side up to lay on a piece of light-colored paper, the plants will separate easily. Each may gently be picked up by a leaf, not the stem, to hold over the individual pot and allow the root to dangle straight in the pot as you use your other hand to fill in with more soil. Press the soil gently around the young plant and try to get it standing tall before you water carefully. This will settle the soil and give the plant a much needed drink. If the stem of a seedling gets broken, it will not survive, but if only one leaf gets damaged or removed, the plant may live.

Place newly transplanted items in shade for the rest of the day to refresh. The second day, a weak fertilizer may be given, but do not drown the "babies." Roots need oxygen to thrive. They should be ready to resume growth if these recommendations are taken. In a few weeks, they need to be hardened off gradually before setting in the garden.

> Alabama A&M University had a planting of 85 basil cultivars in 2004 and invited the Master Gardeners to come to see them. This was an experimental planting to be used in treating type 2 diabetes.

It is a good time to sow dill and parsley in the garden. There is the Italian or flat leaf parsley that chefs prefer. It is not well represented in the marketplace, so you will probably have to get seeds and grow it yourself. It needs the same care as curly parsley. A close relative of parsley is chervil, also sowed at this season or in fall. It has a delicate flavor that can enhance salads. It is seldom added to cooked foods and is considered "gourmet" parsley. All of these

Chervil Seedling

Chervil Leaf

develop a tap root. They do best when planted where they are to grow. Cultivate the soil and scatter some seeds, cover them lightly and water gently. The seedling leaves are easily identified. They are long thin leaves and both come up and separate at emergence. They thrive in the cool weather of early spring. If you purchase these plants, be sure to untangle the tap root, if possible, as you set them out.

Remember that rabbits really love parsley, dill and chervil but hate it when they meet cilantro. Many humans feel that same way about cilantro. It is love it or hate it and is an acquired taste. I learned to like it because it adds much flavor to Mexican cuisine. These herbs are good to grow among vegetables because they attract bees and other beneficial insects to pollinate your vegetables.

If you are planning to use dill seed heads in pickle-making, be sure to sow it in the garden six weeks or more before you sow the cucumbers. The seed heads will be ready when the cucumbers are in abundance or if earlier, just cut off that seed head and you will soon get a second one. Recipes that call for dill weed indicate the use of the leaves — while those that just say dill, usually mean the dry seeds. When the dill has formed mature seed heads, gather stems and hang upside down in a paper bag to dry. All that fall will be saved and you will have plenty for sowing or using in this form. Storing in a closed container in the refrigerator, along with your other seed packages, will keep them viable for one year or perhaps two. If you wish to have the leaves for cooking in winter, they are easily frozen by placing in a plastic bag, removing as much air as possible and putting in the freezer until needed. No blanching is required. Be sure to label them. Herbs that are frozen look very much alike.

Dill will germinate later in the season if kept constantly moist until well established. This will be a challenge in hot and dry weather but is possible with much attention to the moisture needs of the seeds and later the young seedlings. (See **Drench the Trench and Directional Seed Sowing in Chapter 6, Variety of Vegetables.**) A loose covering of pine straw or compost will keep moisture in the soil to some extent. Dill may reseed in later years in your garden, but usually does not become a weed.

Herb plants grown in the greenhouse or in your house should be gradually hardened off before setting outside. Don't just decide that they can stand cooler temperatures and bright sunlight all of a sudden. They may succumb to the shock or dry out in a few hours and be lost. There will still be some cold weather, and this process of hardening off must be gradual. (Plants bought from the nursery or big box store have already been exposed to outdoor conditions.) Those seedlings that you have grown are very tender and first should be placed outdoors in the shade for a few hours. Try to do this on a calm and cloudy day. Increase the time outside each day and gradually expose them to bright sun. After a week if the temperature is above freezing at night, leave them outside overnight, but in a place where they will not be eaten by rabbits. Gradually the plants will become stronger and sturdier and then they will be ready to set in your garden on a cloudy day or late in the evening.

> It was July and a visitor said he wanted to see my vegetable garden, so I invited him to walk around the outside of it and observe how well the plants were growing. There was scarcely a weed in sight. He said that he had worked for Chase Nursery in previous years, so I assumed he knew all kinds of plants. When he saw my unfenced rows of peonies, he asked "Are those peonies?" and I confirmed that they were. He walked on further and saw those tall fern-like plants that were now about six feet tall. "Is that dill?" I gently told him, "No, it is asparagus." I didn't go into the details of dill growing only two feet tall and having umbels of white flowers that later became the dill seeds. But I was quite amused that a person who had worked in horticulture didn't know dill from asparagus. We all should try many different plants to acquire a wide range of experience and be able to help others to do likewise.

## Setting Out Plants

Dig the planting hole and remove any clods or rocks and pour some water in the bottom of the hole before tipping the plant out of its pot. Those six-packs from the garden center probably have roots filling each cell. Cut the pack apart to get the roots out without damage and carefully set the plant into its new home. Do not set it deeper than it grew in the cell pack unless it has become tall and lanky. Often plants with bare stems will grow roots along the stem when planted deeper. Observe your new garden plot each day and tend to watering as needed. After a few weeks of establishment the plants will not need as much care. (Yes,

> **Spring Gardening**
>
> This is the introduction to a lecture I gave on "Spring Gardening:"
>
> Now is the time to start your spring planting. Find an old car seat spring. Dig a hole in the chrysanthemum bed. Press the spring firmly in the hole. Cover with Alabama red clay. Sit back and wait for rain. Then your garden will spring up – but that's great, because that's where you want those "cushion" mums to grow. Now get an old spring from a mattress and plant it in your flower bed. "Bedding" plants should spring up. Surely you want to plant a watch spring in the herb garden, for that is where you want the "thyme" to grow. If you live in the country as I do, you might want to plant a leaf-type spring – the kind found in very old pickup trucks, for a "truck garden." You know, lettuce leaves, spinach leaves and such. But, enough of this foolishness. Let's get serious. Oh yes, do hot peppers get hotter if planted near hot springs? Or does ice plant grow best by cold springs?

gardening is like having a baby: it needs lots of care and training when small, but the results will be gratifying!)

Spring teases us before it really arrives. If a cold snap is predicted, have a few clay pots ready to put over your seedlings for a night or two. Plastic film does not give good insulation from the cold and when the sun shines, your plants will be boiled if it is not removed immediately.

## • APRIL •

This month is busy in the garden. Cut off old tops of sage down to new clusters of leaves found growing inside the plant. Sage, although a perennial, is not a long-lived one. Many times roots will form on branches that lie on the soil and take root. Sage tends to creep across the garden.

Lavender is showing signs of new growth and flowers will appear in June. The first bloom stalks will be vigorous and when picked for drying, will prune the plant somewhat. Lavender may have new plants that layered and rooted without your assistance and these can be dug and potted or transplanted to a new location.

Cut back the velvet sage (Salvia leucantha), if it is planted in your herb garden, when you see new growth arising from the old plant. A bit of fertilizer of some form is helpful in getting things started. Sow seeds of annuals, especially basil, if your soil is good and you can water them if no rain comes. However, many small herb plants are too delicate to survive a heavy rain and are best set out as transplants. Spend some time reviewing your notes from last year. Those dormant plants that are slow to emerge in spring may be just where you had planned to plant something new.

Late April is planting time at last for all of those seedlings you raised — even for tender things such as basil, marjoram and summer savory. The topiary you have in a pot may be taken out of doors for the summer if you have not had lots of trouble with scale and mealy bug pests. Keep it in a protected location and remember to water when no rain occurs. If it is about sixteen inches tall or maybe more, it is time to pinch out the topmost growth for the "lollipop" shape. Keep the trunk tied securely to the stake that gives it support, but not so tightly as to girdle the stem. Women have given up girdles; we should let our plants do the same!

Trim off any side shoots that are appearing and pinch the ends of the side branches so they will grow fuller. You can place the pot inside a larger pot, with moss or plastic peanuts between the two pots for insulation, to protect roots from extreme heat. If it is where it could be blown over, put rocks in the bottom of the larger pot. Wash the whole pot and plant with the hose before bringing it back indoors or in the greenhouse for the winter. If growing vigorously and roots have grown out of the bottom of the pot, it will need a larger pot.

## Herbs for Shade

If you have mostly shade, you can still grow some herbs. Mint will thrive in heavy shade. Just keep it in a pot and don't let it get away. Many of the medicinal herbs are best grown in shade as they were found growing naturally in woodland areas. (Medicinal herb use is not discussed in this book.) Parsley and dill will grow without full sun, and there

---

### Recipe
**Herb Butter**

Soften one stick of unsalted butter. Add 1/2 teaspoon of lemon juice. Now choose no more than three herbs to add flavor. Approximately 1 tablespoon of each fresh herb finely chopped, or 1 teaspoon of dried is enough for this amount of butter (or margarine). Take into consideration that some herbs will overpower others. Parsley is excellent because it combines well with many others such as basil and thyme. Consider using parsley with chives and French tarragon. Try summer savory or marjoram with chives and parsley. The combinations are unlimited. Form into an attractive shape and let your butter "age" in the refrigerator for several hours before using so the flavors can meld. By experimenting with the basic idea of using herb butter to season vegetables, or just on bread or unsalted crackers, you will learn more about their flavors and the ones you prefer.

are others that will do well in partial shade. Some that I have grown in that situation include thyme, cilantro (coriander), French tarragon and chervil. Plants that are customarily used for seasoning food may not be quite as flavorful when grown in shade so just use more of each one. We can always test their flavor by making herb butter.

## • MAY •

This is a delightful month and herbs are showing rapid growth. There are many that can be grown from seeds planted now. Rains will be frequent and if your soil is reasonable, germination is easy. Look for those volunteers of basil and thin them. Each plant will need about two feet of space and those seedlings may be a mixture of several kinds that you had in the previous year. Nevertheless, they all repel deer. Transplant some wherever you see deer tracks. Herbs are excellent plants to use where deer are a problem. They are not much eaten except for parsley and dill.

Full sun is best and a soil not especially rich in nutrients will make for stronger flavor. Good drainage is necessary, especially for perennial herbs in winter. When you are setting out young plants, remember that they need space to mature although if you have not given them space, you will continually have to cut them back. However, that may be the whole point in growing them.

Harvest can usually begin by mid-June. The perennial ones will be ready before June and some you will want to harvest for their flowers, such as lavender. Lavender x intermedia 'Provence' is the one that seems most hardy in our climate. Gather the flowering stems when only a few blooms are open to avoid much shattering. If you do this in early morning, the bees will not be so bothersome. Hang bunches of 10 or 12 stems upside down in a warm dry dark place for drying.

There are many lavender cultivars with different colors of flowers, different growth habits and even different leaves. One of these is dentate lavender meaning that the leaf edges are serrated. It is sometimes called Spanish lavender (Lavandula stoechas). It has a stubby cluster of tiny white blooms that appear early in summer. The pink-toned petals (really bracts) protrude from their calyxes and hide the blooms. It is considered an annual but survived several winters in my well-drained garden.

This plant with very fragrant leaves grows about 14 inches tall. It is seldom

> • Herb Day at the Huntsville Botanical Garden is held on the second weekend of May. There will be tussie mussies for sale and many things to see and taste.
> •

found in the market place, so mail order is the best place to look for it. They have been found at the Huntsville Botanical Garden's annual spring plant sale. French lavender is an unusual plant. It also has large bracts but has leaves without indentations. The tiny white blooms are scarcely noticed but, as in the Spanish lavender, the showy pale lavender bracts reflex above the insignificant bloom. It is also tender and makes a good potted plant. There is much confusion over the classification of these two types of lavender, so if you see one that you like, just buy it, protect it from freezing and not worry about the nomenclature.

Lemon scented and flavored herbs are many. Lemon grass is not hardy in our area and must be protected from hard freezes. It is used mostly in Asian cuisine and is in the herb garden at the botanical garden in Huntsville. My favorite lemon scented herb is lemon verbena (Lippia citriodora or triphylla). This is marginally hardy in our area and grows four feet tall in one season. The stems are square and delicate racemes of tiny white blooms appear late in summer. The leaves, which arise in threes instead of twos as in most plants, are dried for tea and potpourri and their flavor and fragrance will last many years. Cuttings can be taken in late summer to be rooted and produce plants to carry over for the next season. If you have kept a plant through the winter, do not be surprised if it drops all leaves as this is the natural habit. New leaves come out in spring and at that time it can be pruned lightly to make the plant bushy and then set in the garden. Allow it plenty of space. It is seldom found locally, so mail order is the best way to obtain it.

Lemon balm, being a relative of mint, is an invasive perennial herb that you should use caution in planting. Bee balm is of a similar habit and also of the mint family. It may have red or pink blooms and of course bees love it, but beware.

Marjoram and oregano are close relatives. Oregano is perennial while marjoram is annual. The perennial oregano, O. heracleoticum is often propagated from cuttings or root division. Most chefs prefer the more delicate taste of marjoram, but in Greek and Italian cooking, oregano is indispensable. O. majorana, grown from seeds that will germinate in eight days, is the annual form labeled 'Marjoram.' It produces just the right delicate flavor for most foods. Either is easily dried for winter use.

O. laevigatum 'Herrenhausen' is an ornamental oregano. It grows very upright to two or three feet and has reddish-purple blooms. It is an excellent dried spike form for dried arrangements, but is not for culinary use.

French tarragon (Artemisia dracunculus) is a much desired plant that never blooms or produces viable seeds. It is propagated only from root divisions and cuttings. The dead stems may remain in winter, but you should mark its location so as not to dig it up before new growth emerges in late May. Good drainage is a must. It needs dividing every three years and the spreading roots can easily be transplanted to increase your supply in early spring. I have had success with it in my garden. Only Russian tarragon grows from seeds and is a noxious weed that you certainly don't want to introduce into your garden. A substitute for French tarragon in hotter climates is Mexican mint marigold (Tagetes lucida). This is a more upright-growing plant than French tarragon and, if leaves are used before the flowering period in late summer, it is a fairly good substitute for French tarragon. It is a half hardy perennial in zone 7, so do not be upset if it dies in a cold winter.

Rosemary will begin to bloom this month and the flowers may be various shades of blue or even white. There are a few trailing cultivars of rosemary, but they do not seem long lived in our area. I find rosemary to be an excellent deer repellent. I cut long branches and weave them into tomato cages and around cages of tall garden phlox in the flower garden. After they have been there a week or two, they dry and some of their leaves will be shed, but whatever remains still prevents the deer from nibbling desirable plants.

Tip pinching of rosemary and many other herbs makes for fuller plants and many more leaves to harvest beginning in late June.

## Preserving Herbs

Just before herb plants bloom, they have the best flavor. Gather them in the morning after the dew has dried, but before the sun has shone on them for several hours. Bring them to the kitchen and fix a basin of tepid water. Swish them gently in the water and pat them dry. (Better yet is to spray the plants with water the previous day and they may not need to be washed.)

**Refrigerator method of drying:**
If the leaves are large, remove them from the stems and lay them on a dry paper towel. Place a second paper towel on top of the leaves and roll them into a loose roll. Do not enclose them in a plastic bag. We want the air to circulate around them. Place the roll on the back of a refrigerator shelf where they will not be disturbed and leave them there for about two weeks.

Carefully unroll the towels and your herb leaves probably will be dry. If not crisp, return to the refrigerator for another week. Let them get to room temperature before placing in a container. They must be crisp and thoroughly dry before storing in a glass jar and placed away from the heat of the stove. It is wise to label the jar including the date and herb. Check the jar a week later just to be sure no moisture has condensed inside it. Your herbs will be ready when needed. Do not crumble them until ready to use.

When you are adding some to a cooking food, take them out of the jar away from the stove and close the jar without steam entering it. If these precautions are taken, your dried herbs will remain flavorful for two years or more. Dried herbs are stronger in flavor than fresh ones, so use only one-third the amount of dried ones when a recipe calls for fresh herbs. Recipes calling for dill weed mean the leaves. Dill seed is usually specified.

**Conventional oven drying:**
Preheat the oven for just a few minutes at the lowest setting. Turn off the oven. Put the herbs in a single layer on a tray with a little space between them. Leave the oven door open a bit. If it smells good, it is too hot. This will require more attention than the refrigerator method. You may need to turn the oven on again for just 30 seconds, several times, to

get the herbs crisp. Small leaved herbs are dried on the stems, and then stripped off just before placing in jars. You may use some of the stems for seasoning of those that have delicate stems.

**Microwave method:**
This is a modern way to dry herbs but requires some experimentation on your part. Place herbs between paper towels and use high power for 45 seconds. You may need to do a few more seconds, but be careful not to let the leaves get too hot or they will taste burned. Time required depends on the amount of moisture in the herb that you are drying and the power of your microwave oven.

**Traditional method:**
Hanging herbs inside a paper bag, that has been perforated to allow air to circulate, is the traditional method or freezing in ice cubes of water are other ways to preserve your bounty, but you may want to try these other methods. As always, be sure to label these treasures. I find it preferable to dry herbs and keep them in a shelf away from the stove, but where I can see them every day. If they are stored in the freezer, they seem to be "out of sight, out of mind" and are seldom used.

Most herbs are added to food towards the end of cooking. The most notable exceptions are winter savory, rosemary and bay leaf. These are added early in the cooking process. Bay leaf is removed before serving the food because of the tough texture. Bay tree is difficult to propagate and tender in our area and must be cared for during winter using facilities that most of us do not have. There are many more herbs to grow but the ones discussed here are the common ones.

> • Some herbs are invasive and some scatter numerous seeds. Be cautious about placing these plants in your garden. (See **Vicious Invaders in Chapter 7, Lots of Lists**.) •

**An Uncommon Herb**

Asafoetida, Ferula persica, is an uncommon herb.

If you have friends from India, ask them about this herb. It is called "Hing" and is used in the powdered form as a seasoning. This is an ancient medicinal herb that was dissolved in water and given in very small amounts as a soothing enema to babies that had colic. Indian friends report that they eat it almost daily in vegetarian foods and chefs of Indian cuisine use it as a substitute for garlic flavor. The fresh root has a foul odor but was used by slaves to ward off evil spirits and promote health when worn in a bag around the neck. My grandmother and mother often spoke of this or I would never have heard of this herb. It is a perennial of the umbelliferae family and can be grown in warmer climates than zone 7a, but fresh seeds are difficult to find. In spring when a plant has matured, soil is removed from one side of the root zone. The root is then scraped so the sap can emerge. This latex like material hardens and is then collected and dried to make a powder. The root is covered with soil again and grown on until the following year. The powdered form is expensive and often adulterated with harmless filler.

## • JUNE •

Everything is growing if the rains came. Keep after those weeds! If you are adventurous, you may try serving a salad with edible flowers. Nasturtium blooms give a peppery flavor and are plentiful but will soon succumb to hot weather. Their leaves may be used also. The pansies are fading fast, but the Johnny Jump Ups will hang on for most of the summer. The star-shaped blue flowers of borage are attractive in any food and have a slight cucumber flavor. Daylily buds can be stuffed with herb-flavored cream cheese for an unusual appetizer.

Start drying herbs for moth preventive bags. Use equal amounts of peppermint, rosemary and thyme and add a small amount of cloves, for this purpose. Hang stems of sage leaves to dry for wreaths. There are recipes for all sorts of herbal gifts. If you start drying your herbs now, you will be doing pruning that will improve your plants, as well as provide the fragrant and flavorful leaves you will need after frost kills these jewels from the garden.

June is the month for weddings and herbs have long had traditional meanings for brides. The lavender may be at its best bloom stage and excellent for fresh wedding use or dried for fragrance use later.

> In 1939 in the United States, aroma therapy became popular. It was a practice of using fragrant herbs to calm anxiety and to soothe nerves. This has aided in the popularity of herbal use and revived the practice of giving tussie mussies to loved ones. An excellent book on this subject is "Tussie Mussies" by Geraldine A. Laufer, a member of The Herb Society of America. The Huntsville Herb Society started selling tussie mussies at herb fairs and they were well-received. Fragrant candles and potpourri as aroma therapy became popular in the 1980s.

Parsley is known as a breath sweetener after eating garlic. Peppermint and spearmint are relaxing teas. If you are growing lemon basil, lemon balm or lemon verbena, try it in your iced tea. Basil is finally large enough for major pruning for salads, but watch for spittle bug foam on the plant — just grit your teeth and crush the monster hiding in that foam. On occasion, a little green worm may attack this herb, but most herbs are resistant to rabbits, deer and insects. Oregano is excellent at this time. Rub leaves of scented geranium or basil on your arms for mosquito repellent. Make some herb butter and learn new flavors. Use summer savory on the green beans and other bean dishes. It is nature's Beano. Keep trimming and using or preserving your herbs. If some plants in your herb garden are looking a little puny, give them a bit of fertilizer. Liquid applications take effect rapidly, but should not be poured on leaves in the hot sun.

## • JULY •

Now is the last chance to sow seeds for harvest this growing season. Keeping the area moist will be a challenge. Prune back overgrown perennial herbs for the last time. However, tip pinching can still be done, up until frost, without forcing new growth that would be winter killed. If the garlic tops have dried up, it is time to dig the bulbs and dry them in warmth for two weeks before taking them in a cool house for future use. Some may be replanted in late September. Most will keep well for several months but if you have an abundance of cloves, freeze some for long term storage. If you have never made herbal vinegar, it is very easy and will add a little zing to salads and other foods in winter.

Make herbal jelly or jam with abundant fruits. Many suggestions for this are found in the Huntsville Herb Society Cookbook "Some Like

It With Herbs" and the later one "Herb Fare." Look for these at the Huntsville Herb Society Herb Fair.

## • AUGUST •

August is the time to keep watering your garden. The lavender may be blooming again and even begin to form new plants where stems are lying on the soil. Watering will help this along. If you find seedlings of basil, you may want to dig and pot them for window sill plants to use in winter. If you have different cultivars of basil, it has been hybridized by the bees and those seedlings are not true to the basils that you planted in spring. The parsley worm has defoliated your parsley and it may or may not recover. Well, there will be butterflies anyway. Take cuttings of lemon verbena, scented geraniums, pineapple sage and other tender perennials that you want for next year. Try rooting them in your house where it is cool and use an old terrarium for the cutting box. There will not be any drainage in this container so keep the soil barely moist. Misting may be needed but with a glass cover and no sun, the cuttings should root. If this is not successful, you always have a second chance in September.

When you have gathered more herbs than you plan to dry and want to keep them for a few days to use, place the cut herbs in a glass of water and cover the glass and cut herbs with a plastic bag.

### • Herb Vinegar

*Recipe*

Pick herbs early in the morning and if they are not free of soil, wash carefully and dry between paper towels. Every trace of water must be removed or the vinegar will be cloudy and not keep well. White or cider vinegar or wine vinegar may be used. Heat it in a stainless steel pan to just below boiling.

In a sterilized pint jar, place about 1/2 cup of slightly bruised herbs. You may add a freshly peeled clove of garlic, dill leaves or seed head, French tarragon or other herbs of your choice. Pour vinegar over the herbs and place a non-metal cover on the jar. If you only have metal jar lids and rings, put a layer of plastic wrap over the jar before screwing on the lid. Shake the jar a little and put in a cool dark place.

Every few days or at least once a week, shake the jar and return it to the storage area. After six weeks, your vinegar should be well-flavored. At the end of this steeping time, strain the vinegar through a coffee filter. Discard the herbs and pour vinegar into a sterilized decorative bottle. At this time you may add a fresh dry sprig of herb for decoration. Use a non-metal cap for the bottle. Use it for making vinaigrette salad dressings, marinades and other such seasonings.

•

> At this time, your basil plants may show dark stems and begin to deteriorate. This could be the result of fusarium wilt disease. It is seed-borne and may be present in the soil. It develops rapidly when wet weather occurs. Plan to plant your basil in another location next year and get fresh seeds to sow.

Place in your refrigerator and they will remain fresh for about a week. This will work for herbs purchased from the grocery store also.

## • SEPTEMBER •

The Mexican sage, also called velvet sage (Salvia leucantha), is beginning to bloom. It makes an impressive accent at the back of your garden with tall stems of velvety-purple blooms that are excellent for drying and are essential for dried bouquets. Although it is said to be tender in our area, it has lived in my garden many years in a protected place with the dead tops remaining all winter. Trim those tops off in late March. This herb is only for decorative use, but well worth the effort to grow.

> If you happen to see the acronym, **GRAS**, in an herb or gardening book – it means **G**enerally **R**ecognized **A**s **S**afe to consume.
>
> This is a status label assigned by the FDA to a listing of substances **(GRAS list)** not known to be hazardous to health and, thus, approved for use in foods.

Sow seeds of cilantro, chervil and parsley. These will germinate this fall and live over as small rosettes until warm weather arrives in spring. You will have these to use before the spring planted ones are large enough to use. Deer will eat the parsley and chervil if given a chance! This is a good time to survey your garden and make notes of what was successful and what was a failure. These records will prove valuable in following years. Make a map of your garden and the herbs that go dormant and disappear can be located again next year. Many times, winter weather removes traces of chives and others without our noticing. If we can locate areas where these grew, there is less chance of injuring them as we set out new plants. If we know where the basil and such grew, we know where to look for volunteer seedlings next spring. If you had more than one cultivar, the volunteer basil plants will not be true to type, but make good deer and rabbit repellent plants in the vegetable garden next spring.

## • OCTOBER •

October is the month of many herb fairs. Plan to go and buy some things you may use for gifts or herbs that can be planted in fall if they are perennials or used as house plants. This is the last chance for harvesting before frost destroys all of the tender herbs and you put the garden to bed for winter. If your lavender has sulked, perhaps a mulch of sand or pebbles will help it survive the winter. Most herbs do better without mulch but a sprinkle of lime around lavender and winter savory can get the soil just right for next year if it is too acid. Dolomite lime is the preferred form and it is slow to take effect.

> Huntsville Herb Society has a herb fair on alternate years at Huntsville Botanical Garden in early October.

Again, most perennial plants, herbs included, do better remaining messy until March. I have had success with leaving the dead tops on scented geraniums many years. It just requires patience to wait and see if in late April they finally come up. Pull out annual plants and keep after those weeds. Just take the cold months to enjoy the things you preserved. Wreaths of dried herbs and flowers are wonderful gifts but require numerous hours to construct. Wait until spring to do any serious gardening.

## • NOVEMBER & DECEMBER •

The garden has gone to sleep and we have time to make gifts of our preserved herbs. Look on the Internet for ideas or get library books to peruse. Hopefully, you dried the herbs you will need and be able to spend worthwhile hours preparing unique gifts for loved ones. Your home will be a place of fragrance as these are prepared. Gather fresh parsley, rosemary and other hardy herbs to use in your cooking and for the presentation of your Thanksgiving turkey. You will probably have fresh sage for the dressing. You always wondered why the men wanted to nap after the big feast. Sage is a sleep-inducing herb and was used as a tea to lull babies to sleep, and evidently works on men also.

> Visit the Huntsville downtown library to see the Huntsville Herb Society Christmas tree and get ideas for making dried herbal decorations to use in your home.

Make or buy a wreath form and cut fresh greens and herbs to decorate your door. Artificial trimmings are nice, but have no fragrance. Boxwood clippings, holly and rosemary sprigs are wonderful for this use. A warning is due. Use small trimmings of rosemary in the dormant season. I once sawed off some large branches of rosemary in winter and the result was a dead plant. Your topiary is now ready to take a prominent place in the holiday décor. Dress up the pot with foil, but punch holes in the bottom and put a saucer under the plant for drainage. Make many small red bows and use twistems to secure them to branches. It will need frequent watering, but don't overdo this part of its care.

> •
> If this were a radio program I would end it with the following:
>
> "Well, it looks like my thyme is up. I would like to thank my sponsor, Basil, my technical advisor, Rosemary, and Ginger, my director. Tune in tumeric (whenever that may be) for another kitchen "caper." Dill we meet again, have a spice day."
> •

If you have a friend or relative who loves plants, a rosemary topiary makes a nice gift. Dried or fresh herbs tied in the napkin ring are a pleasant addition to your table décor. When there is a fire in the fireplace, throw some discards of herbs on it for added fragrance and memories of your time spent with these wonderful plants.

Closing words of advice: I was only able to write this chapter in winter months because I have kept detailed notes on my gardening work for many years. I strongly advise you to keep a garden journal. Make a map of your garden and use labels to mark the places where there are plants that go dormant in their off season. If you would like to join the Huntsville Herb Society, information about meetings can be obtained at Huntsville Botanical Garden. There is a wonderful herb garden there that is maintained by the Huntsville Herb Society.

CHAPTER • FOUR

# Beneficial Bugs, Birds, Bats and Biochar

There are many beneficial insects, bacteria, fungi, birds and animals.

### The Lady Beetle

The first insect we think about is the lady beetle. We learned the verse "Lady bug, lady bug fly away home. Your house is on fire and your babies will burn" as we blew our breath down the indented trap in the soil. It was really the larva of the ant lion that is similar to the lady beetle larva. The adult ant lion is a small flying beneficial insect similar to the dragonfly in shape. In the dry soil of West Texas where I grew up, we often had this experience but the ant lion lives only in dry climates and sandy soil where the trap can be made. We never see this indentation in our soil because the lady beetle lays eggs in clusters on plant leaves where they hatch, pupate and become the larva.

Lady bug larva

The primary food of the lady bug is the aphid, and when very dry weather comes, if there are not plenty of aphids, the lady beetle in both the larval and adult stages may starve to death. When the weather is conducive for the aphids to multiply, the lady bugs soon will arrive also. The larval stage of this insect is about one-eighth inch long and black with several orange spots across the body. If you have read the article

> In early fall, when visiting the Astronomical Observatory on Mount Palomar east of Los Angeles at an elevation of 5,000 feet, I saw millions of lady bugs clinging to tree trunks awaiting spring. (An enterprising person first collected these beetles and started the business of selling the insects to gardeners.) This telescope was the largest in existence in 1948 and was cast at the Corning Glass Works in Corning, New York. It had been in use 20 years at the time of our visit in 1968.

about aphids as pests, you will not worry about the lady bugs and hope they will not "fly away home" before eating lots of aphids.

Lady bugs may be purchased by mail and it is important to release them in the evening when there is moisture and aphids are numerous. Otherwise they may fly away to some other garden where the food is plentiful. The Asian lady beetle (See aphids in **Chapter 5: Gremlins in the Garden**) was introduced early in the twentieth century to combat pecan aphids. It has proliferated and become a nuisance because it invades our homes. As with the beneficial lady beetle, it does eat aphids and is beneficial. It prefers to spend the cool months inside our homes and seeks any small opening to do so. You will not likely be able to exclude this insect, so just capture them with the vacuum cleaner and destroy them or release them. I am convinced that the same bugs enter the house again, so we bag them up and give them to the garbage man.

> We once had a praying mantis as a "pet" for a few hours. It was on our front steps and it watched us as we watched it. We fed it a tiny morsel of ground beef and it took it from our outstretched fingers and ate it. My children were fascinated by this insect behavior.

## Praying Mantis

The praying mantis (sometimes referred to as mantid) is well known for eating garden enemies. This large insect will eat any insect, even their own kind, if available. They are interesting to watch because unlike any other insect, they can turn their heads from side to side. The insect uses its two front legs to capture prey and it is said that the mantis can grasp a fly before the fly has time to spread its wings to escape. It will capture bees and other beneficial insects to feed its voracious appetite. The tan-colored egg case is well camouflaged and appears as

Praying Mantis

an enlargement on a stem. We clean up our gardens in the fall and probably destroy many mantis egg cases in the process. If you find an egg case in the fall, try to leave it where it was placed.

We sometimes see the insect known as the Walkingstick. It belongs to a different family of insects from the praying mantis and is not a beneficial. This insect was given the right name, as it appears as just another stick on a plant until you see it move. It does not prey on other insects, but eats leaves of oaks and other deciduous forest trees.

Walkingstick

## Green Lacewing

The green lacewing is a good insect to have in your garden. You have to look carefully to see it because its wings are nearly transparent and folded above its body in a vertical position when at rest. This insect with golden eyes is only one inch long and is a predator of aphids and scale. You may observe the egg case before you see a mature lacewing.

Green lacewing

The female lays the egg at the end of a slender threadlike stalk about one-half inch in length. This hangs, or sometimes, stands on a leaf surface. You are inclined to ask yourself "What is that tiny white thing hanging onto a leaf by a silk-like thread?" The silk-like thread holding the egg may be placed in rows. After the larvae hatches and feeds on aphids, it goes through the second stage as a silken cocoon before becoming mature. All stages of this insect prey on aphids.

## Syrphid Fly

An excellent pollinator that is probably in your garden without your knowledge is the syrphid fly, also known as the hover or flower fly. Syrphid flies are active in

Syrphid fly

catching and eating smaller insects and lay eggs in colonies of aphids. Members of the fly family, unlike bees, hold their wings slightly spread over their body when at rest. If you see a fly with a longer body than the honeybee and four yellow bands across its back that are separated at the center, and working the center of a flower, it probably is a syrphid fly. It closely resembles the honey bee but does not have a stinger. Unlike bees, they do not form colonies and make honey, but feed on nectar, aphids and mealy bugs. The best way to entice these beneficial insects is to grow flowers that they like, such as the flat blooms of yarrow and the daisy family.

To encourage all of these beneficial insects, it is good to provide the plants that they prefer. Even before your garden is producing vegetables and fruits and the flowers are in full bloom, they will be there to help things along by eating many pests. By eliminating weed and brush piles, you will discourage many pests. Keep in mind that when you use most chemical insecticides, you are killing off the "good guys" along with the "bad guys."

## Beneficial Spiders

Beneficial spiders are present and we do not notice the small ones. The large webs of the orb weavers are seen after a humid night when the dew  is sparkling on the filaments of the web in the early morning. The female exhibits yellow and red bands on its body and legs. She may vibrate the web when you are near in an effort to frighten predators away. A new web is constructed from the center to the outside edge each day. You may notice a thick white zig zag stripe in the web. How interesting that the male spider spins this part of the web. Many small flying insects are caught in the large web and devoured by the resident female.

In fall, she will lay her eggs in a tough brown paper-like case at the edge of the web, then drop to the ground and die. The eggs hatch and the tiny spiderlings over-winter in the case without nourishment until spring, when they emerge and scatter to make their webs to capture food. There are many other beneficial spiders that are working to catch moths at night and some that are in the grass and eating small insects as they are trapped in tiny webs.

## Birds

Birds are the gardener's best friends. Yes, they eat fruits and peck vegetables, but overall they are beneficial. When they peck your tomatoes, they may just be thirsty, so put out a source of shallow water for them nearby before this bad habit begins. The perching birds and song birds that spend the whole year here are some of the best ones to encourage. In winter, they are observed sitting in branches of deciduous trees and suddenly flying to the ground to catch small insects. These birds seem to have excellent eyesight. In spring and summer, they need even more insect food to feed their young.

Migrating birds come to our area for the summer from distant climates where they have spent the winter. **Purple Martins** returning to nesting sites arrive in February. Locations near ponds where mosquitoes and other water insects thrive are favored. However, they do not really consume many mosquitoes. They eat only insects, including dragonflies, other flies, wasps, hornets, and stink bugs, and spend all daylight hours in pursuit of their food. If you live in a rural area, you may be able to attract these migratory birds with a multi-compartment martin house. Gourds are the traditional houses and if vegetative gourds are not available, plastic gourds may be placed in groupings on a 20-foot high pole. A method of lowering the houses for cleaning or replacement is an advantage.

We observe these day-flying birds on guard and there are others that are present after dark. One of these is the **chimney swift**. There are several nests in the downtown area of Huntsville where old chimneys remain standing on historic buildings. These beneficial birds are welcomed by nearby residents. In another area of Huntsville are the **night hawks** that are attracted to lights where swarms of insects are gathered. All

> When we first put up a tray-type bird feeder at our new country home, we expected to see birds enjoying the feast while we enjoyed watching them. No bird seemed to notice. I had grown sunflowers the past summer and had saved a few heads. I tied a sunflower head to the feeder. Suddenly the birds came and discovered that there were plenty of seeds on the feeder. We "taught" those country birds to use a feeder and they entertained us.

of these bird friends migrate to South America for the winter. As the days grow short, insect populations recede and "no insects, no birds" of these species.

Most birds are on guard duty for the garden during the day, but **owls** are on duty after dark. We seldom consider them as predators. They are known for eating rodents and living in barns and hollow trees. Mice and their kin are likely to taste your corn, tomatoes and melons while you sleep. Are there any outdoor cats in the neighborhood? Owls are known to attack cats, so most cats are kept indoors for their own safety. Be glad. No digging in your garden for use as a litter box. We welcome owls to keep mice and even insects out of our gardens.

The Huntsville Botanical Garden has an extensive birding area and owls aid in the control of harmful insects and small animals. Owls occasionally live in wooded areas of the suburbs. They are predators of mice, small birds and insects and rely on their sense of sight and hearing to find prey. They can hear the rustle of a rodent and, possessing flexible neck bones, turn their heads to see it. Owls swallow their prey whole at the nest site and later regurgitate the undigested remains in pellet form. Upon examination, these pellets are found to contain bones, fur, teeth and insect exoskeletons.

## Bats

> Bat Conservation International has headquarters in San Antonio and educates the world about these valuable animals.
>
> Website: www.batcon.org.

The bat is the only flying mammal, and we think of them as Halloween ghosts, but they are beneficial. Some are smaller than a hummingbird and weigh only as much as a penny. The only bat that feeds on blood is the vampire bat of South America that sucks blood from cattle. By studying the saliva of these bats, a medicine to prevent the coagulation of blood was developed. Most colonies live in caves and some migrate to Mexico or South America in winter.

Bats are responsible for the pollination and spread of such foods as mangos, avocados, dates, figs and cashews. Their droppings have supplied nitrates for gunpowder and fertilizer known as guano. Bats find their prey by using high pitched clicks called echolocation. (Dolphins and submarines use this same method of contact that is called sonar.)

In North Alabama, most bat colonies live in one of the 3,000 caves in the area and hibernate there in winter. The largest bat colony in the world is in Bracken Cave on the outskirts of San Antonio, Texas. This huge colony migrates to Mexico in late September and returns in May. As early as 1902, people in the area realized the importance of bats as beneficial mammals to control insects and were installing bat boxes in their yards.

On their nightly forays, each of these millions of bats eats five times its weight in insects and benefits farmers by destroying thousands of root weevil moths. The numbers of bats are declining because of chemical use, diseases, human intervention and lack of knowledge about these important animals that produce only one "pup" each year.

---

Some of our blueberry customers like to stay out in our field after dark to look at the stars and enjoy the sights and sounds of nature. One evening, an older couple from an Asian country who did not speak English, were here with their daughter and her husband. They came up to our barn to pay for the berries they had picked before going back to the city.

The frogs in the pond across the road had tuned up their "rain song" and the father asked his daughter, "What is that sound?" He thought it was frogs, but she could not confirm it. She asked me what made the sound and I told her, "Yes, it is frogs and toads singing for a mate across the road in the pond and we often see frogs and toads here in our blueberry field." This information was relayed to her father. Then I explained to her that frogs and toads spend the early part of their lives in water as amphibians, but they eventually become land dwellers. She thought about this a few moments. She had seen our small group of bats flying above the field seeking insects and asked me, "Do frogs fly?" I assured her that the flying creatures were bats that lived in a cave on the top of the mountain, behind our house. I then explained to her that frogs and toads could hop across the road to our field in the dark of the night, when they are active, and live in our field to catch insects. Later, they would go back to the pond where they would mate and produce eggs that would become tadpoles in the pond, before shedding their tails, and turning into frogs and toads.

This was new information to the young woman and her parents. I hope it did not lose meaning in being translated to another language, for the benefit of her parents.

## Other Beneficial Creatures

Let's get down to earth and see what beneficial creatures we may have not thought about that reside there. We are familiar with **toads, frogs and lizards**. Some, classified as amphibians, live in water part of their lives and on land at other times. We know about tadpoles and their eventual transformation into toads and frogs. All of these need a source of water to survive. They are all beneficial in that they eat insects and other small garden pests such as slugs.

Eastern fence lizard

When the warmth of spring arrives, lizards come out of hibernation to bask in the sun and hunt for food. Our most common lizard is the **eastern fence lizard**. They will sit on a rock or other place where their dull coloration blends in and wait for long periods to catch any insect that chances to land nearby. I have watched one capture a stink bug, so they do not object to the bad odor and probably foul taste. If you have a few in your garden, protect them from the cat or small boys who try to catch them. Fortunately, lizards sense when danger approaches and swiftly take cover.

During summer and also during late fall, after mating, the female makes an indented place in loose soil and backs into it to lay her clutch of white eggs, each the size of a jelly bean, then pushes soil over them. In a month they will hatch into very tiny replicas of their parents and feed for a few weeks until cold weather forces their hibernation. Mature lizards hibernate during winter under rocks or fallen logs when no food source is present.

Skink

We also see the **skink** with several blue stripes reaching from head to tail. It can shed the tail to escape capture and grow a new tail. They have the same general habits as the eastern fence lizard. (It has been proved that if a cat eats any part of the skink, it may lose balance and suffer other nervous system problems.)

**Toads** also seek a safe place to hibernate during winter. They may burrow two inches into loose garden soil to wait for spring. Be careful doing spring tilling and digging that you do not inadvertently spear one of these valuable bug eaters. **Frogs** usually do not live in gardens. Many spend their adult lives in moist areas and we seldom encounter them.

Toad

An inquisitive child wading along a creek may turn over a rock and find a **salamander**. The best advice I can give is "Do not touch!" These slimy black amphibians have a body covering that will cling to your hand for hours and only the strongest abrasive soap will remove it. Salamanders devour slugs and snails and hide most of the time.

**Snakes** have a bad public image, but they truly are beneficial and part of the food chain. We have several non-poisonous ones that live near our barn door and although we have tried several times to evict them, they refuse to move out.

## Biochar

Most of us have not even heard of biochar. It may hold promise for the future to eliminate the effects of harmful materials on soils. When we see "char" as part of a word, we immediately associate it with "charcoal." Biochar is a product of burning waste of vegetable or animal origin to make a form of charcoal that absorbs objectionable elements from soils and "purifies the soil," so to speak. Experimentation has been ongoing for a decade or more in universities around the world. In Africa, rich soils as much as six feet deep have been discovered and are believed to have occurred from ancient peoples' practices of burning plant residue and burying it while flames were present, to produce rich soil. They found that the crops that followed were exceptionally good. This was not the same as "slash and burn." When that practice occurred, the people moved to new areas to cut down and burn vegetation to prepare new planting areas.

Biochar may absorb carbon dioxide and methane gases and sequester these harmful gases for centuries, preventing their effects on global warming. In the process, heavy acid soils, such as are found in rice paddies and similar situations, can be improved and nutrients important to crops are retained and released, as needed, for the plants grown in soil that has been treated with this product. It will make acid soil less acid and, although it will improve nutrient content in neutral soils, may harm acid loving vegetation. Areas that have been mined, and where farm practices produce animal wastes that are difficult to dispose of without harming nearby water, may be reclaimed by the use of biochar.

Proper preparation of the raw materials is essential and cannot be performed by the home gardener. In burning plant wastes, we produce harmful gases and release them into the air. Any person who has built a campfire or burned trash, knows that oxygen is necessary for combustion. In production of biochar, high temperature is required and absence of oxygen takes place so charred material of a certain quality is produced. This method of burning is called pyrolysis, defined as "chemical change brought about by the action of heat." Production of biochar is somewhat like producing alcohol in a still, except that the resulting gases are captured to use as fuel — biofuel. Raw biochar in small pieces (that have more surfaces) have been soaked in compost tea to impregnate them with soil microbes that are beneficial to plant growth. In this way, less nitrogen fertilizer is needed and the soil is enriched without adding chemical fertilizers. The resulting crops have increased in growth and health and provided improved harvests.

The briquettes that are used for outdoor cooking are not usable in the garden because of harmful binders used in their production. I am not a scientist and do not have a degree in chemistry, but these are my impressions of this discovery. Biochar, as a soil enhancer that will have an impact on global warming, may be the idea of the future. I suggest that you investigate this further through the University of Washington by using the website http://pubs.wsu.edu.

## CHAPTER • FIVE
# Gremlins in the Garden (Pests)

### Afraid So

Did the car hit my mailbox?
Did the squirrels get in the birdfeeder?
Did my tomato plants freeze?
Did the cat throw up on the new lawn chair?
Did the cut worm chew off my pepper plant?
Is that a dead chipmunk in the fish pond?
Did the fire ants sting your ankle?
Is that snake poisonous?
Did it bite the dog?
Did the raccoon get my corn last night?
Are the eggs broken?
Did the mice eat my peanuts?
Did the horse step on your foot?
Did it rain on that fresh cut hay?
Did the rabbit get my beans?
Did the birds peck the peaches?
Did the possum get the figs?
Did the moles tear up the lawn?
Is that a skunk caught in the Havahart trap?
Did the Japanese beetles eat the rosebuds?
Did it rain after I sprayed herbicide?
Did the lawnmower hit this tree?
Did the deer jump over that fence?
Are those Asian lady bugs in the window?
You burned the trash and then the barn burned down!
I'm going to throw away my rabbit foot and four leaf clover.
Will I ever have any good luck? Maybe so, now that this is over.
— *Mary Lou McNabb, 2016*

We need to consider the habitat necessary for garden pests and see if we can eliminate some of it and still have a garden. While we were living out in the high desert of California away from any neighbors, I had an opportunity to see what reasons there were for the absence of insects. There was no rain and no water except what humans supplied for their yards in town.

We were surrounded by cacti and a few drought-proof plants such as bougainvillea and pomegranate trees that were producing fruits in abundance and were growing in abandoned places. I was surprised to see these two thriving. There must have been a few pollinators, possibly hummingbirds, for the pomegranate trees to have those fruits. I had a few tomato plants and petunias in my sandy yard. I watered them daily and they grew well, but never an insect was present.

We had lizards, snakes, scorpions and tarantulas. Those last two are not really insects. Spiders have eight legs, while insects have only six. There are some others that we consider insects, such as millipedes, that have many more legs. We will let the entomologist classify those. Chemicals that kill insects do not kill spiders. Here in our area, we welcome the "harmless to humans" spiders and only dread the black widow and brown recluse. If in your garden you are lucky enough to have garden spiders and lizards, rejoice! Always, we welcome toads and birds. A few harmless snakes are permissible too. You learn to live with them and steer clear of their habitat.

Insects need moisture, habitat, food and absence of predators and harmful chemicals. Remember that not all insects are villains — there are several that we should welcome into our gardens. Pictures are the best way to learn who is welcome and who is not. The damage caused by harmful insects can give you good clues as to who is chewing or sucking on your plants. We will not consider household insects as they are for the exterminator to worry about.

I well remember visiting a friend's garden in New York State many years ago. She had asked me to come see it because there were scarcely any tomatoes or squash or other vegetables, although the plants were growing well. She had attacked every insect and disease at the first hint of trouble and not even a butterfly was to be seen. There was a large collection of pesticides in her garage. I believe that she had killed off most of the pollinators as well as the harmful insects.

Remember that you can do more harm than good with chemicals!

## Aphids

The most common pest is the aphid. They manage to color themselves for camouflage and are often called plant lice. Female aphids may proliferate without mating in spring. The females may survive the winter as live pests or the eggs, laid in protected locations the previous year, will hatch in spring. Wonder of wonders — all eggs will hatch into females that do not need mating to occur before they produce young that are all (guess what?) females. This is called parthenogenesis.

Lady beetle, ants and aphids.

Spring is always wet to some extent and young plants are growing tender new growth that is a favorite from which aphids suck juices. Here they have all their needs in abundance. "Quick! Henry, get the Flit" was the call to action many years ago. We have many more options now. Because aphids are sucking-type insects, you must get the insecticide on the pest because, while sucking juices, they will not "eat" any of it. Aphids tend to hide on the underside of leaves or on stems and are difficult to hit with the spray nozzle.

Lady beetles and their larvae eat aphids. Ants "farm" aphids to get the honeydew that they secrete. Often there is a black residue on host plants, from the honeydew that indicates their presence. There are the "botanicals" that are used by organic growers, and we should take a lesson from them. Some of the most common are insecticidal soap, Bt (Bacillus thuringiensis) and Bk (Bacillus k, Bacillus thuringiensis kurstaki), diatomaceous earth, rotenone and pyrethrum. Even crushed egg shells can be of some use to prevent slugs and snails from attacking your plants and using other means of barriers can help. Always start

Hornet nest
Photo by Robert McNabb

with the least potent treatment and try to consider the beneficial insects.

Among the beneficial insects are bees of many kinds, hornets, yellow jackets and wasps. You may just learn to avoid them as they look for prey to feed their young or insert their eggs into caterpillars feeding on plants. Remember that swatting at them only causes them to become aggressive and that the color of your clothing (yellow) and any fragrance that you are emitting will attract them. Keep calm and slowly move away. Try to determine where their nests are located and stay out of the "line of flight" — the path between where they are working and the nest.

If the plants are not wet with dew, early in the morning is a good time to tend your plants as the insects have not awakened yet. Late evening is likewise a good time. You will notice that many insects move to the top of plants late in the evening so they will get the first rays of the morning sun and "wake up." Get 'em while they sleep!

Lady beetles have been recommended for ridding your garden of aphids. If your house faces west and is of a light color, you are a likely victim of the Asian lady beetle that was introduced in the early 1900s to combat the pecan aphid. It has become a household pest because it seeks the inside of homes to wait out the winter.

Because the aphid is so numerous, we (maybe) should help the lady beetles. The Asian type has a different mark just behind the head in the shape of a black "W" (or "M" if you are looking in the other direction.) If they have invaded your home in years past, you will know that they cluster in groups, and if you disturb them they sometimes pinch and also emit a foul odor. Their feces will be left on windows and even drapes.

They can enter in very small gaps and exclusion is the preferred way to avoid them. Unfortunately, most houses are not sealed enough to prevent their entry. You can remove them with the vacuum cleaner and then discard the bag or empty them outside and hope they do not return in a few hours. They seem to have no predators and the beetles and their larvae eat aphids. Are they beneficials or pests? You be the judge.

## Fire Ants

Fire ants have invaded our area in recent years and you just have to keep battling them. The hot water treatment sounds good, but does not work for very long. Often any chemical treatment only causes them to move to a new location. They steal seeds if you have not covered them with soil and watered the rows. If you have been

Fire ants

stung, you know how painful that is. This is a good reason to always wear socks and closed shoes outdoors. Baits are the best approach to this problem and new products are frequently introduced. Early spring is the best time to treat the nests. Ants have waists, but termites do not.

## Grasshoppers

Grasshoppers are a difficult garden pest to control. Hitting them with any spray is nearly impossible and catching them is also. Grasshopper bait is available. It is sold as a treated wheat bran flake that the grasshopper ingests. It contains nosema, a tiny protozoan that infects the grasshopper. When the female lays eggs, they are already infected with the microscopic protozoan and will not hatch. If grasshoppers were not so mobile, they could be completely eliminated. This bait does not harm birds or any other creature, so is environmentally acceptable. It is good to keep tilling your garden, if not perennial, especially in fall and even winter if the soil is dry enough. Freezing weather will also get rid of eggs of other insects. Fortunately, grasshoppers do not get too troublesome until fall. Spinosad may be effective but will require several weeks of treatment to eliminate these pests. Birds can catch them. Encourage the birds.

## Click beetle

What is that elongated brown beetle that can turn itself right side up and makes that clicking sound as it does this? That is the click beetle. Larvae are wireworms and are often found in new gardens that

Click beetle

were sod until recently. In the larval stage it tunnels into gladiola bulbs, potatoes, radishes and other root crops and kills grasses and vegetables by eating their roots. The eggs are laid deep in the soil and hatch into a small wireworm, an elongated flexible hard coated worm. This worm molts many times over the course of three to six years. After this stage, it pupates for three weeks before becoming the mature beetle in the fall. The beetle hibernates in the soil until the following spring when it emerges to begin eating leaves. The best way to reduce the population of wireworms is to let the soil lie fallow for one season and till it frequently to turn up the worms so birds can find them. If it lies fallow over winter, many wireworms will freeze or become food for the birds.

## Cicada

The thirteen- or seventeen-year locust (cicada) is a pest. The experts declare that it does not do much damage, but it has pruned the tops of many shrubs when the eggs are laid by the female inserting them under the bark with a row of splinters remaining behind. The topmost branches break off and fall to the ground. The larvae from these branches burrow down deep in the soil to await their next emergence. There is not much that can be done to combat this pest. Collect and destroy the fallen twigs. That may help if the eggs have not yet hatched and the larvae burrowed into the soil.

## Cutworms

Cutworms are the enemy of young plants. They are the grubs of several night flying moths and live under ground except when cutting off your seedlings or newly set transplants. They are thick bodied and usually in a "C" shape when unearthed. The best treatment is to protect your young plants with a collar of some kind. I have used a strip of aluminum foil to crimp around the stems of many plants and it has worked quite well. Each strip should be large enough to insert into the soil at least an inch and fold around the above ground stem

> •
> My daughter called me to ask why her new plants were dying. I asked her how they looked and she said, "They just lay down and died." I knew then they had been cut off by cutworms.
> •

above the soil two inches. If just crimped around the stem, the foil will release with the enlargement and toughening of the plant stem and the cutworm will be unable to cut it off. When I pull up tomato plants in late summer, the foil collar is still there, but has been sloughed

Cutworm

off by the plant as the stem grew larger in diameter. Some gardeners have used pieces of cardboard rolls on which various paper products are rolled. I find the foil collar easier to use as slipping a roll of cardboard around a rather husky plant becomes a problem.

If you are sowing seeds, it is a different situation. Try to turn the soil several times in fall and winter and again in spring a week or two before you plan to sow seeds to expose the grubs and let the birds have a feast. You may even get the **squash vine borer larva** while trying to control the cutworms. They also winter over as a pupa or in a silk-lined cocoon two to four inches below the soil surface. If you find grubs as you turn the soil, kill them. The grubs may be hiding in the soil nearby and you will need to do lots of soil turning to get even most of them. Some gardeners have had good luck by sprinkling hydrated lime, not ground limestone, around their rows of seeds. Even though rain comes, the lime prevents cutworms from crossing it to cut off seedlings. Hydrated lime will burn wet hands. Diatomaceous earth or those finely crushed egg shells that you saved all winter can be sprinkled around the seedling row to identify it as well as prevent slugs and snails from consuming your seedlings.

Skunks dig up lawns and gardens to get grubs and do more damage then the grubs. I expect our recent invasion of armadillos is digging for grubs also. If you just ignore the fact that there are cutworms, you may not succeed in growing plants by direct sown seeds.

## Bugs

Some insects are classified as bugs. The word "bug" is in their name. They have piercing mouth parts on the heads of their bodies. This tells you that they are sucking type insects and the insecticide must hit the insect to kill it. Fortunately toads, lizards, birds and other predators eat some of them. Most have wings that are folded flat over their bodies when at rest. A few of the most injurious to our gardens are the squash bug, squash vine borer, leaf footed bug, azalea lace bug, boxelder bug, chinch bug and various stink bugs. There are a few predator bugs that are beneficial.

Adult squash bug

## Adult Squash Bugs

Adult squash bugs over-winter in buildings or trash and emerge when the weather warms. At this time, your squash plants are germinating and growing well and blooms will soon form. The squash bugs mate and females will soon lay eggs on your young plants. We may cover our young squash plants with row cover when they have just begun growth, but when blooms begin to form they must be uncovered so pollination can be done by bees. The orange eggs are laid in clusters usually on the underside of squash leaves and are found next to leaf veins. A few minutes spent rubbing them off and crushing them will help to eliminate some of these pests. The eggs soon hatch and the nymphs will inject their needle like mouth parts into the plant cells causing a wilt disease and killing the plants.

If you go to your garden early in the day you may find numerous squash bugs of all sizes on stems below the leaves and may be able to kill many of them as they seek to hide. It is difficult to hit the insect with spray, so diligent hand-crushing is the best tactic. Wear gloves. A gradual metamorphosis takes place as the nymphs grow and shed their skins to become mature. When crushed, they release a bad odor and are called stink bugs, but this is not the correct name. Any insecticide used must hit the insect to destroy it. Insecticidal soap, neem or pyrethrin may be used and are kind to the environment.

## Leaf-footed Bug

The leaf-footed bug is most prevalent in late summer and fall. It is easily identified by the leaf shaped hind legs. The sucking parts of this bug inject damaging substances into tomatoes, beans and cowpeas, among others. This causes the fruits to begin to deteriorate and spoil and also spreads diseases. The leaf-footed bug and other such bugs congregate on the tops of host plants including flowers, in the evening to be ready to feed when morning comes. Look for them there in the evening and crush all that you find. I know this is unpleasant, but who said all of gardening was all pleasure? As before, these are controlled by hand-picking or spraying with a botanical such as insecticidal soap or as a last resort with carbaryl.

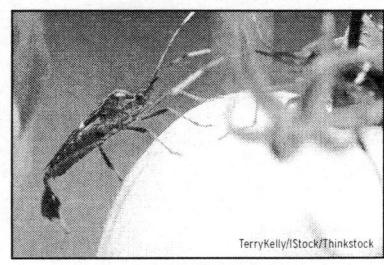
Leaf-footed bug

It would be good if we could just cover our plants with floating row cover, but the bees or other insects must pollinate the blooms before we will have fruits. The male blooms of many vegetables come first and then the female blooms with the immature fruits behind them are later. Pollen must be transferred from the male bloom to the female bloom before fruiting will occur.

## Chinch Bugs, Azalea Lace Bugs

Chinch bugs are primarily lawn pests. Azalea lace bugs are injurious to those shrubs and usually are introduced by bringing in the insects on infected plants. They suck the leaves from the underside and cause them to appear grayish and stippled. They will weaken the plant and are not easy to eradicate. It is difficult to spray these plants and cover the underside of the leaves. The soap sprays are the best botanical to use, but in desperation, a systemic pesticide may be necessary. Because there are so many insecticides now in use, the azalea lace bug is almost never seen on plants that are for sale.

> A recent addition to organic insect control is Spinosad. It can be used on edible crops and some mixtures include this insecticide, a fungicide and a miticide. It must be ingested to be effective. The smaller local garden shops will have it before the big box stores. Recently there has been much interest in organic gardening and most of the big box stores will eventually provide these products.

## Spittle Bug

The spittle bug may attack your annual plants in late summer. I have only seen it on basil plants. It is easily noticed when you see a ball of foam in the leaf axil of a plant. The insect is safe in the spittle and the best way to remove it is to use your fingers to crush the spittle. You will feel the insect, so just crush it. (It takes guts to be a gardener!)

## Mealybugs

Mealybugs are mainly greenhouse and houseplant insects and may be found on the above ground parts or roots of plants. They have waxy coatings that protect them from insecticides and, at one stage, are a small fly. They are sucking insects and hard to eradicate. Only a systemic chemical would kill them. The best solution is to just discard the plant.

## Scale Insects

Common scale on leaf

Scale insects are another slow moving pest. They are often in large numbers before we notice them. The very small males fly to the wingless females and mate and reproduction takes place on the host plant. For the most part, they are greenhouse pests, but occasionally are found on rosemary branches in the garden. In the greenhouse, they may infest cacti and succulents and are round brown patches sometimes in groups. They can be scraped off with a brush (dipped in Malathion) or rubbed off of tender plant surfaces

Oyster shell scale

with your fingernail. Dormant oil or lime-sulfur sprays may be effective or just removing branches that are infested is helpful. Many scale insects look like miniature oyster shells or are just round in shape. The presence of honeydew-attracting ants is another warning of their presence. As with mealybugs, when scale appears it may be best to just discard the plant.

## Cucumber Beetles

Cucumber beetle

Spotted and striped cucumber beetles are a threat just when your vines are thriving and you are getting lots of fruits. They are quick to fly away when you approach. You will recognize their presence when they begin eating blooms of cucumbers, beans and other plants. Because they are chewing insects, an insecticide that remains on leaves, and will be eaten, is successful. Not only do they chew leaves, but also spread cucumber wilt and cucumber mosaic diseases.

In recent years, seedling plants of the cucurbits have been available in pots and are usually set out to get a head start with this vegetable. Cutworms will get them if not protected with collars. The collars we use also may deter the insect from laying eggs next to the young plants. If direct seeding, covering the planting area with row cover will allow them to get established before the beetles can attack.

The latest idea to control flying insects is to cover the row with netting similar to that found in a fabric store to make ballet tutus for costumes. It is green and will not protect from frost, but will deter most flying insects, depending on their size. (Aphids may be an exception.) The adult beetles have spent the winter hibernating in surrounding areas and we cannot expect to kill all of them. After mating, the female lays eggs next to plant stems. White larvae hatch and feed on cucumber roots below the soil line and infect the plant with diseases. Larvae then pupate and soon emerge as adults. Watch for these insects and use pyrethrin-rotenone spray or dust to eliminate this pest. Fortunately, these botanicals are toxic only to fish. If you have not previously grown your

> There are some cucumber cultivars that will produce fruits without pollination, and they theoretically could be grown under row cover the whole season. It is too hot and humid and the plants spread too much to do that in the average garden. Cucumbers are commercially grown in plastic-covered high tunnels where no insects are present. There is no need for insect pollination, and air currents could spread pollen if needed. Most of the blooms on these specific cultivars will be female and have a small cucumber just behind the inflorescence. I have had success with these in my outdoor garden.

cucumbers on a trellis, give it a try. They will be clean and require less space and are easier to find and harvest.

## Flea Beetles

Flea beetles have a similar life cycle to cucumber beetles. They also winter over as adults in surrounding areas and as soon as their preferred foods appear, they will attack them in great numbers. The beetles are black and one-sixteenth inch in size. They riddle leaves with tiny holes and jump away when you approach. They are very prevalent on eggplant and other members of the solanaceae family. Eggs are laid in the soil and hatch into larvae that feed on root crops before pupating and becoming flea beetles. Rotation of crops will help as will fall and spring cultivation. Exclusion is good, but the blooms must be pollinated if you are to get fruits. Rotenone or Spinosad are the preferred treatment. Leaves must be covered on both sides with the insecticide.

## Mexican Bean Beetles

Mexican bean beetles are very injurious to beans as well as other plants. The adults winter over in trash and grasses and emerge in late spring. They are kin to lady beetles, but are larger (one-third inch) and of the convex shape and yellow orange in color. The adults mate and yellow-orange eggs are laid on the underside of bean plant leaves. They especially favor lima beans. Soft yellow larvae hatch in 5 to 14 days depending on the temperature. They eat on the underside of bean leaves spreading diseases and leave a lacy pattern of veins. They also feed on stems and pods and there are several generations in one summer. Rotenone spray must reach the underside of leaves to be effective.

Planting your seeds as early as possible so the crop can be harvested before the beetles arrive is a good strategy, and destroying all plant debris when the crop is over is also necessary. If you plan to use the vines to enrich the soil, bury them deeply as soon as pulled out. A follow-up crop can be planted immediately, but not of the bean family.

## Thrips

A tiny insect that does much damage is the thrips. (Yes, that is singular and plural form.) It is usually not noticed until flowers or onions display the damage that has been done. You may not even realize that you have them until you notice some streaks of gray tissue in onion stalks and tops falling over before the onions are mature. Thrips over-winter in onion scales and also in debris remaining in the garden, therefore it is important to clean up the vegetable garden in fall.

Flowers such as roses, peonies, gladiolas and chrysanthemums are their favorites besides the damage caused in the vegetable garden. Flower petals will show streaks of dead tissue and in gladiolas, there may be stripes of white and you may think they are part of the normal bloom instead of damage. However, the blooms will soon dry up. Also, thrips spread spotted wilt virus to tomatoes, dahlias and other flowers.

Mouthparts are able to rasp and pierce plant tissue. They are especially prone to attack yellow and other light-colored flowers and are so small that their damage is observed before the insect is apparent. (Many years ago the test was to blow tobacco smoke into a bloom and the thrips would emerge and be seen.) They have thin bodies that are one-sixteenth inch long and usually dark brown or black. Wings are folded over the torpedo-shaped body.

Tilling the soil in fall, destroying plant debris from the past season and eliminating weeds near the garden seem to be helpful, but no botanical insecticide will effectively control them. In desperation, sprays or dusts of carbaryl or Malathion may be applied, but must spread down into the leaf axils and buds of plants. Crop rotation will help as it does with many other insects and diseases. Any bulbs that you have dug and suspect of having thrips, that are to be stored over winter, should be soaked in Lysol solution (1 1/2 teaspoons in one gallon of water) for three hours, then allowed to dry thoroughly before storing in a cool dry location.

## Mites

Mites are not insects but are of the order Arachnida. This order includes the mites and other spiders such as web weavers, chiggers and daddy longlegs. Mites have eight legs instead

Mite

of the six on insects. The mite that is most prevalent on garden plants is the red spider mite. As before, chemicals that kill insects do not kill spiders. Plants may look sickly and have yellow leaves. You will notice webs underneath the tops of plants. A closer look with a magnifying glass will reveal the tiny spiders. Washing away the underside and topside of the leaves with a forceful spray of water will help some, but does not kill all of the mites. Sprays of insecticidal soap will work quite well and neem oil also is recommended. Sometimes it is better to just discard the infested plant.

## Caterpillar, Worm

Tomato hornworm

Everyone is interested in preserving the butterflies. When I see a butterfly, even though it is beautiful, I think "there is a worm in your life cycle." (The terms "worm" and "caterpillar" will be used interchangeably in this article.) Butterflies fly only during daylight hours while moths fly mostly at dusk or night. Another difference is that butterflies hold their wings upright while at rest and moths hold their wings flattened over their bodies while at rest providing good camouflage during daylight. Butterflies and moths do not eat plant parts, but use a long tongue (proboscis) to sip nectar and do some pollination.

The **tomato hornworm** is easily noticed and will eventually become a night flying moth. If you are out in the garden late in the evening, you may see the hummingbird moth, with a wingspan of two or three inches and feathery antennae, that is the parent of the tomato hornworm. The eggs, which we never notice, hatch into leaf-chewing worms and pupate inside a cocoon that winters over in the soil. This is another important reason to clean up and till the garden in fall. Hand-picking is effective to some extent but other measures may need to be employed.

Several wasps are predators of the caterpillar. If you observe white egg cases on the back of a caterpillar, just leave that one to be destroyed by the wasp larvae that are in these egg cases. Birds also eat many of these caterpillars. Spray of Bt (Dipel and Thuricide) are recommended controls. If you go to the garden late in the evening or early morning, you will find the caterpillars at the top of plants where they can be removed and killed. (Yes, they have tough skins and dropping them on the soil and stepping on them may be needed.)

The **squash vine borer** is the larvae of the clear winged moth that resembles a wasp. It has an orange and black marked body but you rarely see it in daylight. Small eggs are laid singly on the underside of stems of squash and other related vine crops and are flat and brown. The larvae hatches and bores into the stem of the squash vine and soon causes it to wilt.

Braconid wasp eggs on tomato hornworm larvae

You are advised to make a hole in the stem where you see frass and kill the borer with a sharp object, then mound soil over the stem to promote formation of roots to sustain the plant. I have never had this to be successful.

Later in the season the larvae will attack any squash fruits that have formed and damage them. Removing and destroying the affected plant will be of some help. Even not planting squash for a season may be necessary, although the borer also affects cucumber and melon crops. Larvae spend the winter in a silk-lined cocoon two inches below soil level.

The most recent idea to eliminate this pest is to dust the stems of the plant with neem dust. This is a plant-based insecticide from a tree that grows in India and is a relative of the chinaberry tree. The larvae will eat the dust and be paralyzed and starve. Neem dust or Neem oil concentrate diluted and used as a spray (it has a bad odor) is believed to be non-toxic to any other insect, fish or mammal.

The most frequently seen pest of the brassica family is the **white cabbage butterfly**. If you want to protect your brassicas from the larva of this butterfly, you should cover the plants immediately after setting out (on a

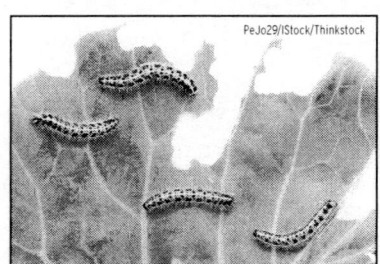

White cabbage butterfly caterpillar

cloudy day when butterflies are not about) with floating row cover. We leave the row cover over the plants for the whole growing season as we are going to eat only buds and leaves of these plants and they do not need pollination. The butterfly has over-wintered as a chrysalis attached to any plant or even a building. It will hatch in early spring just when we are setting out the brassicas. Eggs are laid singly, in the hundreds, as the butterfly briefly alights on the underside of the brassica leaf to deposit each tiny yellow egg. If you do not get the row cover on immediately, the butterfly will lay eggs and the larvae will be protected by the row cover and safe from any predators. (It happened to me — once!) The velvety-smooth green caterpillar hatches in a week and begins to feed. A skeletonized leaf of the turnip or mustard plant is evidence of this very destructive worm. It eats into the heart of the broccoli plant and is hidden until the vegetable is cooked and served. There may be as many as six generations in a season. Rotenone is a possible control, but Bt is also effective. Destroy pulled up plants and next time put the row cover on immediately.

The **cabbage looper** is also a serious pest of all of the brassica family and many flowers. The parent is a white moth. The female lays single small greenish white eggs on upper surfaces of leaves. These soon hatch and the larvae feed for two weeks or more before spinning a cocoon that is attached to a plant leaf while the larvae change into the moths. The larvae of this insect, which produces several generations in a season, often feed on geranium flower buds. Bt is the best solution to this problem. The minute trichogramma wasp is a predator of the larvae.

Parsley worm

The **black swallowtail butterfly** is the parent of the **parsley worm**. Some gardeners grow many parsley plants, so butterfly larvae will have plenty of food. Maybe the gardener too will get some parsley. The worms eat voraciously and can strip a parsley (or dill) plant of all leaves in a few days. If you look closely, you will see parsley worms of all sizes on a plant. The larva is black, green and yellow striped and has a forked horn on one end of the body. The dilemma is whether to kill some or all or let them become butterflies. The larvae pupate in a chrysalis attached to the host plant over winter or sometimes the butterfly lives through a mild winter to begin the life cycle again. Perhaps we should leave it all to the birds. Hand-picking is usually successful if you don't want any butterflies.

The **monarch butterfly** has been an environmental subject in recent years. It has a migrating habit that has produced much tourism and is truly fascinating to study. The adults fly over water for hundreds of miles from Canada and the eastern United States to the forests of Mexico to winter on trees in that warm climate. Other swarms of them winter on trees on the coast of California at Pacific Grove near Monterey. It is awe inspiring to see large flocks of these insects clinging to trees in their wintering grounds. The following spring these adults begin their flight back north to the summer location and on the way they will mate, lay eggs then die. It takes three to four weeks for the egg to become a butterfly and as this period passes, the vegetation farther north has developed enough to support the next generation of the insect. One of the mysteries of nature is that the new generation knows how to proceed to the summer location.

Monarch butterfly

Gardeners have been encouraged to plant native milkweed as food for these generations when they are making their migration and also as food for those that stop to summer in various parts of the flight path. Our perennial butterfly weed with orange flowers (asclepias tuberosa) is of the milkweed family. It is not as prolific as the wild species but is eaten by the monarch larvae. Both the caterpillar and butterfly are foul tasting and poisonous. They have bright markings that birds and other predators recognize and avoid. You may see our common viceroy butterfly and think it is the monarch, but the monarch is larger and has several yellow spots on the forewing. The larva is banded with black, white and yellow stripes and a pair of

Monarch butterfly larvae

black pointed appendages on both ends of the body. It forms a chrysalis with noticeable gold dots on it before showing the colors of the butterfly just before emerging as the adult.

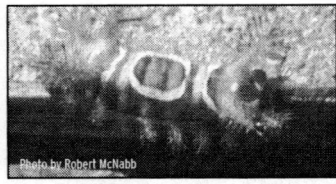
Saddleback stinging caterpillar

A word of warning to observers of caterpillars: there is a **saddleback moth larva** that has stinging hairs on it. It feeds on many orchard plants and forest trees. When seen, it is usually about one inch long. Beware! You will know if it has touched you. There are a few other moth larvae that also have stinging hairs on them, but are rarely found on garden plants.

Few of us grow corn because it requires much space to grow enough to get good pollination and full ears of kernels. When growing corn, plant several short rows. The tassels provide the pollen that is carried by wind to the silks to cause kernels to form. If the tassels are destroyed, blame the **Japanese beetle** or the **corn earworm**. Some cultivars have protective husks and are partially resistant to the corn earworm. It also attacks tomato fruits and bores into the stem end of green tomatoes. The moth that flies on cloudy days and also at night is seldom seen, but has brown fore wings and white hind wings with dark spots. It lays eggs singly on the host plant, which may be a geranium bud, tomato plant, sunflower head or corn tassel. The larva soon hatches and begins to feed on the tassel and then the ear of corn.

Oil spray will deter the earworm if applied when silks are small. I expect there are GMO (genetically modified organism) cultivars of corn being planted that are immune to this pest! Summer oil can also be applied to sunflower heads as a deterrent as this worm frequently attacks sunflower blooms. Deep tilling of the soil in fall and spring will be of much help in uncovering the pupae. The worms are found inside a green or ripening tomato and destroy the fruit. You may find tomatoes with ripe skins, but empty of inside tissue hanging on the vines because this worm has eaten them from the inside. Birds feed on the worms and, during the pupa stage, two to six inches deep in the soil, moles eat the pupae. (Is this the only good thing moles do?)

## Nematodes

Nematodes are one of the most difficult pests to eradicate. Prevention is the best deterrent but that is after the fact when they have invaded your garden plot. Review the past history of your garden plot and try to remember when and how the nematodes may have arrived. Did they perhaps come in soil on a plow or other implement? Or in a plant you received from some other garden that brought them? The most effective treatments have been discontinued due to environmental hazard and we are left with treatments that are only partially successful. Marigolds are probably the best and easiest solution. We must grow them in abundance and turn the plant residue into the soil while the plants are still green and growing. The nematodes did not suddenly appear in your soil, and it may take several seasons to get rid of most of them. Experts advise letting the soil remain fallow or covering it in hot weather with clear plastic to heat up and "cook" the pest.

Very recently, a biological treatment has been discovered. It is the myrothecium verrucaria fungus grown in a laboratory. It must be the dead form of this fungus, as the live one causes plant disease. The dried dead fungus and the medium in which it was cultured are applied as a dry formula. It may cause skin or eye irritation and precautions must be taken in using it. It is worked into the upper three to six inches of the soil at any season, even when plants are growing. (If used in the vegetable garden, I am not sure I want to eat this substance.) It is harmless to beneficial nematodes. Yes, there are a few beneficial ones out there.[1]

How do I know if I have nematodes? Because they are microscopic animals that usually invade plant roots, you may just have sickly plants until you pull up the plants and look at the roots. They are called "root knot nematodes" because the roots they have invaded are distorted with knots. Remember that roots of bean plants have a knotty shape because they absorb nitrogen and "fix" it in this manner. Tomato plants do not have this type of root, nor do most other plants. Most plants will not thrive if nematodes are in their

[1] "What's Wrong With My Plant and How Do I Fix It?" David Deardorff/Kathryn Wadsworth. 2009, Timber Press.

This resource contains many pictures and recommends only organic controls.

roots. They will be sickly no matter how you fertilize and spray them. Pull up a few and study their root systems. If you suspect nematodes, try the marigold solution first. This will involve not growing other plants for one season in the affected area of your garden.

There are also foliar nematodes that affect chrysanthemums. The leaves will be yellowed and curled and no insects are in evidence. Of course a systemic insecticide can be used on nonedible plants. But do not plan to grow vegetables anywhere you have recently used a systemic material.

## Sow Bugs or Roly Polys

Sow bugs or roly polys are a common sight in the greenhouse and in moist places in the garden. They are easily recognized because they roll up like a bb shot when disturbed. They eat decomposed plant parts and sometimes eat seedling roots. Although we consider them insects, they have seven pairs of legs and instead of the metamorphosis of insects, the young are held in the body of the female for two months before being released. It takes about a year for this creature to mature. They are easily crushed in the greenhouse when found under pots or other damp places. The solution is to eliminate their hiding places as much as possible. Diatomaceous earth or crushed egg shells may help some.

## White Fly

The white fly is a major greenhouse pest and is also hard to eliminate. It is particularly fond of tomato and pepper plants. In the vegetable garden, they create havoc for a whole season. We hope they are not present in any plants that we buy. They are very tiny but proliferate in a short time. They are found on the underside of leaves where they suck plant juices and cause yellowing. When the plant is moved or shaken, swarms of tiny white flies will scatter about before landing again. If you ever notice them on new plants, wait until dusk and slip a plastic bag over the plant and pot without the flies escaping. Seal it and just discard the whole thing. If they get started on indoor plants, you are in for a bad time.

There are sprays that kill them, but they have to be used at 10-day intervals for several weeks. Sticky yellow traps have been used, but they are not completely effective. Lacewing insects are predators. Incarsia formosa is a parasite of the white fly and may be ordered from specialty companies. Before you bring a new plant into your house or greenhouse, quarantine it for a week in a different room, away from other plants to be sure no insects are present.

## Japanese Beetles

Japanese beetle

Japanese beetles have plagued us for many years. They were not present in my area until people started bringing in sod from other parts of the state to have instant green grass. This is a prime example of an introduced pest becoming a major pest. Before 1912, plants could be brought into our country with a ball of soil, but a law was passed in that year making this practice illegal. Now there is plant inspection and only licensed growers in other parts of the world are able to bring in plants growing in "soil." The beetle has even arrived by airplane. It was found in Sacramento, California in 1961, but measures were taken immediately to eliminate it and it has disappeared from the west coast.

It must have the right soil moisture and other conditions to survive. The female lays 30 or more eggs in sod before dying. Eggs hatch in about 10 days and the grubs begin feeding on grass roots. When cold weather arrives, they burrow down 8 to 10 inches to wait out the winter. When spring comes, the grubs return to eat grass roots until May when they pupate and become the adult beetle. The beetles are especially attracted to roses and many other garden flowers. Fruiting plants such as raspberries, grapes, peaches and others are much favored. Grubs infest lawns and destroy roots. It has been a practice to treat lawns with milky spore disease inoculation, but it will take several years and community-wide cooperation to make a big difference in their numbers. The beetles are colorful and drop off of plants when you approach. Predators do not bother them due to bad taste and odor.

A few years ago, it was suggested that you spread a white sheet under plants and try to knock off the beetles. This will result in some "harvest"

## Japanese Beetle-Proof Plants

Ageratum (houstonianum)
Annual Baby's-Breath (gypsophila elegans)
Perennial Baby's-Breath (gypsophila paniculata)
Begonia
Boxwood
Caladium
Celosia
Columbine (aquilegia)
Coral Bells (heuchera)
Cornflower (Bachelor button, centaurea cyanus)
Coreopsis
Daisies
Dusty Miller (senecio cineraria)
Forsythia
Gladiola
Hellebore
Hydrangea
Lady bells - adenophora
Larkspur
Lavender
Lily (They eat flowers)
Love in a Mist (nigella)
Pansy (viola)
Poppy (annual kinds only, for our climate)
Snapdragon (antirrhinum)
Strawflower (helichrysum)
Sweet William (dianthus barbatus)
Verbena
Veronica
Vinca (annual periwinkle)

•

but how are you to dispose of them if they do not fly away before you can gather up the sheet with them inside it? We found a better way. Early in the morning of a cool day, you may be able to capture some in a gallon milk jug with a wide opening cut in the top. Place it under the place where they have been "roosting" overnight and stir the leaves a bit, and if you have done it right they will fall into the jug. You will have to keep shaking the jug to avoid letting them escape. Hold your palm over the opening while you are looking for more beetles. Now that you (hopefully) have some of them in the jug, how do you get rid of them? Well, we found a good solution. Cover the jug opening with plastic wrap, put it on the side in the microwave and zap it for a few seconds on high. There will be lots of activity for the first few seconds, but it is soon over and all are dead. Rush it to the garbage can to get rid of the odor. Yes, it is cruel but it works.

I have only discussed the most prevalent pests in this book, but there are many more that plague the gardener. If we knew of all of them, we probably would not try to garden at all! The solutions that I suggest are environmentally safe for the most part. Insecticides are required to have on the label the word "Caution" for the mildest ones and "Warning" for more powerful ones, and this is a clue of their strength. In the past there was a more lethal category using the word "Danger," but products with this label are not available to the general public at this time. Those without either of these words on the label are considered very safe. The letters "OMRI" refer to ratings given by the Organic Materials Review Institute indicating that they are acceptable for certified organic culture products.

> **References**
> - "The Gardener's Bug Book" by Cynthia Westcott, Fourth Edition, 1973.
> - "The Audubon Society Guide to North American Insects and Spiders"

Look carefully at your plant and observe what type of damage has been done to identify the culprit then you will know how to approach the situation. There is much information on the Internet about various pests and correct identification is needed before you take any measures to correct it. When using any pesticide, observe the conditions on the label and measure as instructed. More is not better and may damage the plant. Wear protective clothing and apply when there is no wind. Never pour any insecticide down the drain or the storm sewer. Use it up somewhere in your garden. Clean your sprayer or applicator when finished.

## Deer and Other Pests

Animal pests are many if you live in or near a wooded area. They were there first and we have invaded their territory. We are doing things that attract them, so we have to take some preventive measures if we are to have a successful garden. The most important part of avoiding damage by all of the wildlife is to take preventive measures before they have raided your garden. They are creatures of habit and the habit follows from one generation to the next.

There are two things to look for if you suspect deer. Are there tracks? Are plants cut off cleanly? Rabbits have sharp incisors and cut stems cleanly. You would recognize tracks because they are small and in two pairs close together. Deer browse on tender new growth and leave ragged stubs. They have large hooves and they are close together where the deer have moved while browsing. If we know which plants are palatable to deer and do not plant them, that is one approach. By planting the unpalatable selections, we will limit our choices but will be able to enjoy the things we have chosen.

> **Deer-proof Plants**
>
> Deer-proof except in dire consequences, when deer will eat almost any plant. Most herbs are not eaten except for parsley and dill. Many herbs are good in the flower garden.
>
> Boxwood
> Butterfly Bush
> Chinaberry tree
> Chrysanthemum (deer eat blooms)
> Clematis (they try it!)
> Columbine
> Crocus
> Daffodils
> Dahlia – maybe
> Dusty Miller (senecio cineraria)
> Ferns of some kinds
> Hellebore
> Foxglove
> Hyacinth
> Iris (they eat blooms)
> Ivy
> Jasmine
> Lantana
> Larkspur
> Lavender
> Mock orange
> Mountain laurel
> Persimmon (they eat the fruits)
> Rosemary
> Salvia (there are many desirable species for the flower garden)
> Smoke tree
> Spanish squill and other spring flowering squills
> Wild flowers of some kinds
> Snowball viburnum (they try it)
> Spirea
>
> •

Some deterrents work for a while until the deer get accustomed to seeing, smelling and hearing them, but they soon learn that these measures are not a threat and move in to feed. There are a few methods of exclusion that may be successful. If your neighborhood allows fences, a high solid board fence may be successful. An electric fence baited with a bit of peanut butter is less expensive, but will be a hazard to pets and humans and is not desirable in neighborhoods. If tree limbs fall on it, the electric shock will not happen. It will not keep other animals such as squirrels from raiding the garden.

An eight-foot tall fence is the only really sure deterrent for deer. It must be sturdy and is a nuisance to have to mow around. There are nearly invisible nets that are made for fencing and these work quite well, but are still a hazard when mowing because the net gets caught in the mower. Posts must be tall enough and sturdy enough to hold them and most are not tall enough after being driven in the ground. Cedar posts are long lasting and can be obtained in most any length. In rural areas these are the best choice. When first placed, you would need to hang strips of cloth or flagging tape four feet high on the net to make it visible to humans, deer and other animals. Fences that are installed from soil level to eight feet do keep out rabbits, squirrels and other small animals. If the base of the fence is a solid material, such as landscape "blocks," the mowing task will be easier. Net fences must be hung tightly to keep them from sagging or the small animals will find a way to get under them. Laying chicken wire on the ground outside a fence may be a help, but it also is a detriment when mowing. A row of double-fencing may work with the outside fence only four feet tall and the inner one being eight feet tall. The most effective and permanent fence is one made of concrete reinforcing wire and eight feet tall. You must consider where to place a gate and if it will be wide enough for the mower and other equipment to pass without difficulty. These suggestions are expensive and require much material and labor to construct.

Let us try to plant deer-resistant gardens. The types of plants that they do not eat have parts that are thorny, sticky, aromatic or hairy.

## Moles

Mole

Moles are the most injurious pests of lawns. They are also the hardest to get rid of. Their tunnels in your lawn are unsightly and after you "walk them down," they may reappear the following day. They sometimes pull grass blades and other leafy parts of your plants underground to line their nests. They are more numerous in wet seasons because their food is more available. They eat the grubs of Japanese beetles and June bugs (that are similar to Japanese beetles except smaller and brown in color.) These bugs are attracted to lights after dark and eat plant parts of deciduous trees and vegetable plants. Maybe the moles are doing us a little good. The application of Milky Spore Disease granules on your lawn and the neighbors' lawns to kill the grubs that attract moles may have some effect, but it will take a few years for it to kill the grubs. Various methods of control such as chewing gum, broken glass and moth crystals in their runs have been used but none have succeeded. (Treating your garden or lawn with "Mole Med" may be successful for a while.)

The only solution that works on moles is to use traps. These are hard to install and must be checked frequently. Exclusion is difficult, but has

> **Mole Relief Mole Repellent** is sold by Gardens Alive Company in Lawrenceburg, Indiana. (www.gardensalive.com)
>
> Mole repellant home recipe covers 300 square feet:
> 1 tablespoon castor oil (laxative)
> 1 teaspoon dishwashing liquid
> 1 gallon of water

been used for raised beds by lining the beds with hardware cloth that has a mesh of half-inch openings. It must be put down before filling in with soil. A new approach has been to treat the soil with castor oil diluted with water. This is expensive and may have to be repeated several times during a growing season. Pre-mixed concentrates have been offered as Mole Relief Mole Repellent and comes as a hose end "water-it-in" container. Notice that the advertising says "mole repellent" and not "exterminator." However, this is not for vegetable gardens and is mainly for lawns. It is sold by Gardens Alive Company. The home recipe is one tablespoon of castor oil (not the kind that has been altered to make it palpable for human consumption, but the old fashioned kind given as a laxative) and one teaspoon of dish wash liquid in one gallon of water. This amount covers 300 square feet and is safe for the vegetable garden. Some articles advise planting castor beans, but they grow ten feet tall and all parts of the plant are poisonous. Another plant that is said to repel moles is euphorbia. It was once included in a wildflower mixture that I sowed and the plants became invasive.

Vole

## Voles

Voles are very small and, unlike moles, they eat plant roots and come to the surface where you will see their exit holes. Mouse traps may be set near their exit holes baited with peanut butter. If covered with a box to exclude light, that will encourage their emergence.

Any garden near a woodland area is going to be invaded by moles, voles and many other destructive creatures eventually, although you may escape for several years.

## Squirrels

You don't have to live near a wooded area to have squirrels. They love your bird seed and can jump and get to almost any feeder. They plant numerous tree seeds in your yard and in flower pots and these often grow. Try placing a layer of pebbles on the soil in pots to deter squirrels. They can be trapped with a Havahart trap baited with nuts, but you may have to release a few birds before getting a squirrel. If you succeed in getting a squirrel, take it several miles away or it may be sitting in your bird feeder when you return. There are just too many of these pests to accomplish good control. Shooting is forbidden in city and town locations and exclusion is almost impossible. Try the newest idea. Tie a few fragrant dryer sheets to short stakes and stick them in the soil in your garden.

## Raccoons

Raccoons are a big menace. Some may be rabid. Many people like to watch them as they bring their young to any dog food left outdoors. People have tried to tame them and sometimes they become so used to humans that they are no longer afraid. Keeping the surrounding area of your

Raccoon

garden cleaned of brush and undergrowth will eliminate their favored habitats, but they have been tracked with radio collars and travel several miles in search of food in one night. They are notorious for raiding corn just before you plan to gather it. With a large Havahart trap, we trapped five raccoons in five successive nights. No, it was not the same one over and over. They were different sizes and were transported to a wilderness ten miles away. I have given up on growing corn for this reason.

## Skunks

Skunks are the ultimate pests. They dig for grubs, drink from the birdbath and eat vegetables. Fencing as described for deer is the best solution. If you are able to trap one using fish flavored cat food or chicken parts, how will you get rid of it without getting sprayed? The experts say that if you cover the caged animal with a light-excluding cover it will go to sleep. Then you can carefully remove the covered cage and sleeping skunk to the back of your truck and take it to a new location. I have never seen this done. You can call the local wildlife authorities and ask their advice. For a fee, they may even remove the animal for you. Be sure to get the cage back!

## Dogs and Cats

Dogs and cats can wreak havoc in the garden. I spent considerable time training our dogs not to enter the garden. They were mostly compliant even when I was not present. Now there are collars and invisible fences that can take the job of training.

Cats think your garden, with its soft soil, is a big litter box and they are attracted to it. Orange peels are said to repel cats. If you have placed some stakes with dryer sheets around the garden, that may send the cats and squirrels elsewhere. If you have a rose bush or two, save the pruned off thorny branches and place them over newly tilled soil. Cats do not like to tread on stickers and will take their "business" elsewhere. When we were temporarily caring for an inside cat, I had to empty the litter box and took it to my flower garden. This chased off the voles for a few weeks. I do not advise emptying the litter box near any edible plants. Because we do not often have a cat visitor and do not have them as pets for the sake of the birds, the odor of the feces and urine was a new thing for the local critters. Fox urine has been used as a pest deterrent but is expensive and quickly loses its effectiveness. We do occasionally see a fox in our field, but it is rare.

CHAPTER • SIX

# Variety of Vegetables

Here you will learn my experiences with asparagus, brassicas, corn, cucurbits, legumes, okra, onions, peppers, potatoes and tomatoes. At the end of this chapter you will also learn about directional seed sowing, a fun idea for kids in the spring, and how I drench the trench to get seeds started.

> Mark Twain wrote in one of his stories: The only way to keep your health is to eat what you don't like, drink what you would rather not, and go to bed before you are ready.

## Asparagus

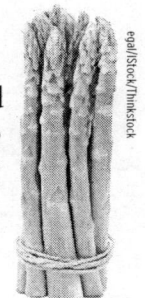

Asparagus roots are available in early spring and it is a good time to get this wonderful vegetable started. You want to buy only male plants as they produce best, and when they bloom no seeds are produced. If you see red seed pods on your plants, you will know they are females and the seeds will supply many plants of unknown sex.

If possible, plant on the north end of your garden in a row going east to west. Dig a trench six inches deep and amend the soil in it with compost. The roots may be dry when you get them and, if so, soak them in water for an hour before planting. Space the clumps of roots about two feet apart. Spread the tubers out over a mound of soil in the trench and cover them with an inch of soil. After a week or two, when they have begun to grow, start filling in the trench. Keep filling in the trench until it is slightly higher than the surrounding soil. This will provide good drainage.

As the growing season progresses, the plants will continue to send up slender fronds. They will grow thicker spears as they age. Do not plan to harvest any tips for a year or two. The roots must get well established before they can survive this treatment. When they have been growing two years, you may harvest six-inch spears every two days. Cut them with a sharp knife just below the soil surface. Do this for only four weeks, then leave fronds to mature and strengthen the root so it will survive the winter and continue to flourish.

As the fern-like fronds grow tall in summer they tend to fall over in windy weather. I have placed a wire fence on each side of my row to keep it standing straight. Plants producing red seed pods should be removed. When frost has killed the ferns, it is time to cut them off an inch above the soil line and discard them. After the second year, you may harvest six-inch spears for three weeks, and after that year, you will have good harvests for six weeks. Give the row compost or other fertilizer in early spring. You will be rewarded with thick delicious spears for many years.

## Brassicas

We will include lettuce and other salad greens of various types here, although they are of the compositae family (plants with daisy-type flowers).

Broccoli covered by Reemay (spun bonded polyester)

**Broccoli, cabbage, collards, kale, kohlrabi, cauliflower, Chinese cabbage and Brussels sprouts** are some of the healthiest vegetables in the garden. All are cool season plants and, because we do not eat flowers or seeds (broccoli-buds only), they can be grown under row cover to protect from all predators above the soil level. Usually they are set out as young plants and may be victims of cutworms. (See **Chapter 5, Gremlins in the Garden**.) Cultivation of the soil before setting out is helpful, but the use of a "collar" is even better. All need a pH of 6.5 and fertile soil.

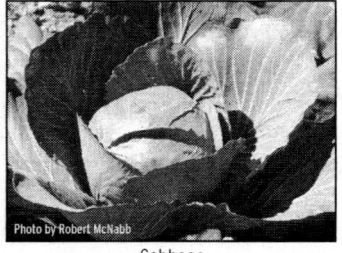
Cabbage

They often produce the best harvests when planted in late summer for fall harvest. Fall provides the best weather for these frost tolerant crops as they mature when it is cool and have better flavor than in spring when they mature in heat. Seeds are started in the greenhouse in late July or early August and it is still very hot. Although seeds germinate easily, growing on to setting out stage is difficult. Be sure to label all flats as all young brassicas look alike, and when setting out, some will need different spacing than others. If the plants are "leggy," they can be set deeper and will grow roots on the bare stem. Probably mass produced transplants are grown farther north where cooler temperatures prevail at this season. Most of these vegetables will mature before really cold weather and often they are enjoyed at Thanksgiving.

Cauliflower

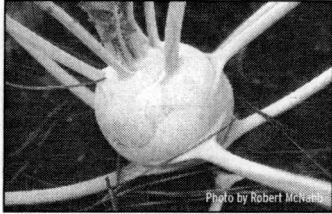
Kohlrabi

In our year of extreme heat and drought, 2016, North Alabama garden shops only accepted one early shipment of these cool weather plants, and few were sold as no gardeners wanted to brave the heat to prepare the soil and keep watering what may not be a good crop.

Spring production of these vegetables is somewhat a gamble. The short weeks of ideal temperature for growing soon turn into summer and insects arrive accordingly. In a cool greenhouse, sow seeds of brassicas in mid-January. Greenhouse ventilation is important when occasional warm days occur. If the soil was tilled and humus added in fall, it is usually dry enough to begin planting in mid-March after birds have had access to insect larvae. As soon as plants are set, with collars for cutworm protection, cover with spun bonded polyester or other row cover so

> My most embarrassing moment was when I had invited the county agent to come and see my brassicas under this cover of spun bonded polyester. When I proudly uncovered the plants, there were dozens of worms and a few butterflies secure under the cover, having a feast on the plants. I had set out the plants and taken a break for lunch before covering them. It was a bitter lesson!

> Pest netting tunnel cover is now available from GardensAlive.com.
>
> It prevents insects and animals from devouring the crop, but is not a frost protection. It would be very useful in hot weather, but requires support to avoid crushing tender seedlings.

no early butterfly or moth will be able to lay eggs on them.

Sudden warm spells in spring may cause the plants to bolt under the cover before they mature. **Kale** is prone to bolting. It is a difficult decision to make. Shall I uncover the plants and take a chance with the butterfly and moth, or leave them covered and hope it is not too hot under the cover? Look around your garden if the sun is shining and see if any predators are flying. Don't forget about hungry rabbits that may munch on them overnight. Perhaps opening the ends of the covering would solve the problem or using the new protective netting. After all of this effort, we certainly don't want to lose them.

You leave the cover over these plants until the day of harvest, so allow for plenty of width to accommodate top growth. Fasten the cover securely to the soil and close both ends so pests cannot enter. It is always better to have too much cover than suddenly realize you do not have enough to cover the whole row.

A fall crop of brassicas is the most successful. Started in July or August, these seedlings will be ready to set out in late September. Often it is still too hot to use a row cover and we are in the dilemma of late spring as stated above. If you can postpone setting out for a few weeks without the plants becoming leggy, there will be a better chance of using row cover. Lightweight row cover or the "pest plant netting" may be a solution. Neither of these is much frost protection. I always apply the row cover regardless of temperature.

> I shall never forget my first experience at the Farmers Market on Cook Avenue. It was the last Saturday before Thanksgiving and I had for sale many buckets of beautiful chrysanthemums and a few plants of collards and cabbage that I didn't have space to plant in my own garden. I set up my booth and when customers arrived, they were most interested in the collards and cabbage. I did sell all of the mums, but was surprised at the interest in vegetables.

Collars to deter cutworms are essential. Suddenly you realize the necessity of labeling these brassicas. **Broccoli** needs to be spaced about fourteen inches apart and cabbages require

*Robert and me in San Antonio – 1946*

*Our children, Ann and Bob, and me in the Wichita garden, 1953*

*Vegetables aren't just for eating! We decorated a few of our favorites for a Christmas card one year!*

*My little garden at a development house in Endicott, NY – 1976*

*Working in my first garden on the Huntsville farm, 1981 – I had just become a Master Gardener in Alabama.*

Robert and I having a bit of fun – dressed as "the farmer and his wife" like the celebrated painting "American Gothic" by Grant Woods.

It's just about berry pickin' time!

Smokey

Blueberry bushes covered in white blooms in April.

Boots

Even the blueberry bushes "dress up" in red for the December holidays!

*Tussie Mussies— the language of flowers.*

*I always enjoyed the opportunity to sell mums at the Farmers Market!*

*My flower garden in full bloom!*

*Hardy cyclamen is a refreshing sight with its beautiful leaves and delicate pink flowers.*

*Grapes on the vine.*

I had fun dressing up sometimes as the "Yarb Woman" for herb lectures to interested groups.

Stunning 'Dr. Henry van Fleet' roses that are disease tolerant and grace our garden in Spring.

Bountiful pumpkin pie!

The beautiful colors of peppers – fresh from the garden!

I love to share the joys of gardening — it was a pleasure to talk with the children at Lynn Fanning Grade School.

spacing according to the mature size. **Collards** and kale may be planted closer together as we pick the outer leaves when harvesting. **Brussels sprouts** will grow slowly and are frost hardy, and when the sprouts are forming on the stem, removal of the top sprout will aid in larger and earlier production. **Cauliflower** is less frost tolerant, and also needs to have the outside leaves gathered and fastened over the forming head to keep it blanched. It is a chance occurrence to produce well in North Alabama.

**Greens** are the easiest to grow and a mixture of various kinds including **kale, mustard, seven top, rape, collard** and others may be purchased. If sowed outdoors too early, aphids may be a problem and if sowed too late, they may not grow large enough to harvest before hard freezes damage them. If allowed to grow until mid-spring, most all will bolt to seed stalks. Late August to mid-September is best for sowing, but it is too hot for a row cover. If sowed too thickly, individual plants may not have space to grow. After germination, thin them out to about three or four inches apart, taking care to remove the cultivars in great abundance and leave a balanced mixture to grow. These are the "potherbs" that are boiled with a piece of fat back and served with cornbread.

58shadows/IStock/Thinkstock
Kale

Round red **radishes**, French breakfast radishes and various other cultivars are grown as spring and fall crops. Given fertile soil, spaced an inch or two apart, they mature in a short time and are best when pulled at the size of an inch or two. In cool weather they are very palatable, but get pithy and strong if heat occurs. The long white winter ones (Daikon) are sowed in fall and allowed to grow in length and breadth even in cold weather and harvested during winter and early spring. These must be spaced six inches apart and may grow to a size of four inches thick and even a foot long if they are not harvested until spring.

> I have seen many a new gardener sow the whole package of radish seeds in a short space and as a result get discouraged when none looked like those in the grocery store. Thinning is very hard for a young person to do because he or she is so proud that all seeds grew. Just quote Henry Field: "Thin vegetables quickly or they will grow sickly." Water the remaining seedlings that will be spaced two inches apart after thinning.

## Beets and their Kin

Beets are cool season vegetables and are available in many sizes, shapes and colors. 'Bull's Blood' beet leaves are being used as a salad green. Sow in early spring, mid-March in North Alabama, and scatter a very small amount of borax (1/4 teaspoon) and some lime if your soil is acid, when preparing a 10-foot row. Young beets are not frost tolerant, but if they have acquired some size before a hard frost, will probably survive. If they germinate in abundance, they may be carefully transplanted and spaced three or four inches apart. Study the seed package and harvest at the recommended size for best quality. A fall planting is often successful depending on weather conditions.

**Beets, Swiss chard and spinach** are of the amaranth family. All prefer cool temperatures, but Swiss chard will do well even in warmth. Seeds are compound. Each "seed" is really a cluster of several seeds and will germinate as a group and need thinning to a foot apart. Some seed companies are separating the clusters so it appears that you are receiving many seeds in the package. If the package contains several varieties, this works out fine. With various colors of stems, red, yellow or cream, they are often used as ornamentals. Leaves, when half mature, are gathered from the outside of the plant and served raw or cooked. New leaves form and can be harvested for several months. If stems have grown too large and tough, they can be cut away and the remaining leaf part can be used. The ribs are either cooked longer or not used.

**Spinach** is very frost tolerant and when planted in September, there will be some harvest in fall. It usually lives through the winter and will produce some good leaves to use in early spring before making a seed stalk. Spinach prefers a little lime for good production but will produce a fair crop in any humus rich soil.

'Malabar spinach' (basella alba) is a summer green that needs a trellis to support the vine. Sow seeds in April, ten inches apart. Use the tender leaves for salads or cook larger leaves to serve with meats. The flavor is intense and develops a glutinous quality when cooked.

## Quinoa

This plant, grown in the Andes Mountains of South America, has become a popular culinary seed, containing protein. It requires a long growing season of cool weather and may be grown in the Southwest of our country, but is of the Chenopodiaceae family, as are many weeds. Probably we should just purchase this food as it would not perform well in our hot climate.

## Lettuce

It is interesting to grow various forms of lettuce and romaine as salad greens. There are numerous Asian cultivars, Pak Choy, Bok Choy, and various romaines that grow in cool weather. There are lettuce cultivars for cool weather and others for warm weather, meaning they will tolerate hot weather to some extent before bolting. All are "leaf" types and 'Green Ice' and 'Red Sails' are two of my favorites. We have developed a fancy for the micro greens that are currently prevalent at the grocer, but we could possibly grow some in our gardens. Mesclun or micro green mixes include many interesting cultivars, some strong flavored and others mild.

If you have a cool greenhouse, leaf lettuce can be enjoyed during fall, winter and early spring. It is best to sow seeds in a community flat and barely cover with potting soil. Given moist soil and light, they will germinate in a few days. After two weeks, they will need to be transplanted to a larger area. I have used long "porch boxes" for planting containers and this has been very successful. Use some compost in the bottom and then fill with potting soil. Space the small plants about six inches apart if you want to harvest mature leaves so they will each have space to grow to that size. If watered carefully, no washing of the harvest will be needed. If micro greens are

> I remember being served a leafy green salad at a Master Gardener conference in Portland, Oregon, several years ago. The Master Gardeners had grown the lettuce and were proud to be able to have it to serve to such a large group. When my plate arrived, I noticed a small worm on a leaf. Being tactful, I didn't mention this, but quietly removed it and squished it in a paper napkin and continued to eat the salad. You do what you gotta do!

desired, direct sow the seeds thickly in a large container instead of doing the transplanting. These are usually sheared off as small leaves and allowed to regrow. They will be rather tedious to gather without leaving sheared off leaves to decompose in the bed. Supplemental nitrogen fertilizer will be needed to encourage a second harvest. As warmer weather arrives, most will bolt to seed stalks.

Growing lettuce out of doors is difficult because so many pests like it as much as we do. Slugs, snails, rabbits and worms all enjoy this crop. If you decide to grow lettuce in the garden, put some mulch such as straw or pine needles under the plants to prevent them being splashed with mud in rainstorms. Choose cultivars that tolerate warm weather if this is done in spring, and choose those that tolerate cold weather for fall crops.

## Corn

All wildlife wants your corn, particularly raccoons. If you live where they are not a problem, have some fertile garden soil, and can get the pot boiling before you harvest those tender delicious ears, then plant corn!

Corn is a heavy feeder and most cultivars produce only one ear on each stalk. In the home garden, it must be sowed in several short rows for good pollination. Wind distributes the pollen from the tassels to the silks. If you plant one long row, you may get a few kernels on the ears, but you will be disappointed in the harvest. The newer cultivars specialize in sweetness and must be planted away (500 feet) from other less sweet or standard cultivars, such as 'Silver Queen.' If they receive pollen from other cultivars, less sweetness will result. The kernels are planted one-inch deep and five inches apart and later thinned to 10 or 12 inches apart in the row. Rows should be a foot apart, or slightly more, to facilitate hilling up and space for you to get between them for harvest. "Knee high by the Fourth of July" was the expected stage of growth in more northern areas, and we hope for some harvest by that date in the south. In North Alabama, this may not be realistic, but in mid-July, you will have some cultivars ready for harvesting.

In dry seasons, "drench the trench" before sowing the seeds and wait until the last frost date has passed or take a chance and plant a week earlier. When stalks get two feet tall, give a supplemental fertilizing and hill up the base of plants to protect from wind damage. When doing this, do not damage roots. You will provide a trench between rows for flooding with water as the tassels appear and later when the silks are receptive to pollen. If roots show after hilling up the rows, fill in with mulch.

> The silks on the ears are beginning to turn brown and harvest is near. Here comes the raccoon! In one night, raccoons can devastate a patch of corn by pulling down ears and chewing on each one before moving on to the next stalk. They travel as much as two miles in search of food in one night. Perhaps you have seen the PBS program showing raccoons with electronic collars that could trace their nightly forays. They seem able to conquer any fence. Keep the dog in the patch overnight or stay there with a gun, if it is allowed in your neighborhood.

All is going well and suddenly the Japanese beetles appear to eat the tassels that are releasing clouds of pollen. Also arriving is the moth that flies in the evening and on cloudy days laying eggs on the silks that will become the ear worms. This worm is also the tomato fruit worm. A few days after the silks appear, as a precaution, place a few drops of mineral oil in the center of the silks or use Neem as a dust or spray. Some cultivars of corn have shucks that wrap tightly around the forming ear, and are less troubled by the earworm.

Many cultivars produce suckers low on the developing stalks and we were advised to remove these. However, now it has been proved that suckers contribute nutrients to the plant and do not need removal. When silks begin to turn brown, harvest time has arrived. Puncture a kernel and if juice squirts out, it is ready. Most cultivars have one or two days when prime ripeness occurs and if left in the field, best quality will be missed. If you want to keep some ears for eating a second day, do not remove the shucks as they preserve the sweetness best when allowed to remain. Store in the refrigerator produce drawer.

## Cucurbits

Included in this family of plants are **cucumber, squash, melon, and pumpkin**. There are numerous insects that prey on them

egal/IStock/Thinkstock

'Cool Breeze' cucumber - two blooms at each node

because they are plants that thrive in warm to hot weather.

**Cucumbers** have been offered as young transplants in recent years and that gives them a head start on the season. They must be handled carefully when setting out, as the root system is not extensive and any loss of it will set the plant back. There are some compact cultivars that can be grown in containers, but most require considerable space unless trellised. Recent introductions include parthenocarpic ones that do not require pollination to produce nearly seed-free fruits. These are grown in plastic tunnels in the off season and can be covered with fine netting to exclude insects in the outdoor garden. Root insects damage them unless the soil is free of these pests. If sowing seeds directly, wait until May when warm soil will permit rapid germination and growth.

Most are planted in "hills," meaning a group of seeds is planted only a few inches apart but not necessarily on a raised area. They are later thinned to two or three plants, choosing the strongest to remain. If a trellis is provided, you may need to help the tendrils get attached to the wire. Always use fencing with openings of six inches, or the cukes will get tangled in the fence and be hard to gather without breaking. Seed packages of the parthenocarpic ones will contain some seeded cultivars for complete pollination. I have considered growing the parthenocarpic cucumbers under fine net to exclude insects. It would require a large cover for these spreading vines, and weed control would be difficult.

If you get cucumbers planted early and they grow well in your fertile soil, many fruits can be harvested before the insects arrive in numbers large enough to cause diseases and damage the plants. Rotating this family of plants to a different location in the garden or planting in a large container may be a better solution to these multiple problems.

**Squashes** are of two major types: summer and winter. Those harvested when young and succulent and eaten cooked or raw are summer squashes, whether shaped round and scalloped (pattypan), elongated (zucchini), or yellow with curved necks such as "crook neck." All of these are best harvested when barely a few inches in size. There are recipes for those that you didn't notice until they grew large, but they require much more preparation. Winter squashes are usually long-keeping ones with hard shells. They are more tolerant of insects and, if sowed in May, will produce alarming quantities of fruits. Butternut and spaghetti squashes are very prolific and sprawl over large areas of the garden. Squash bugs do attack them, but the stem borers cannot do much if any damage. These must be left to ripen to the proper color and allow the shell to harden before harvest by cutting with a section of stem. Kept in above freezing temperature, they will remain edible for many months. The extra-large winter squashes, such as banana, blue Hubbard, acorn, Turk's turban, cushaw (seldom grown nowadays but grows well in hot climates) and others are grown more successfully in cooler climates although the demonstration vegetable garden at the botanical garden has grown a few.

Butternut Squash

Giant pumpkins are grown in cooler climates and prizes are awarded for the heaviest ones often weighing as much as 1,200 pounds. Many smaller pumpkins are grown by Tate Farms, near Huntsville, and a festival is held each September and October with many activities for the whole family and many unusual varieties of pumpkins are for sale. If you succeed in growing pumpkins (the small pie pumpkins are most successful), remember that animals will break them open and feast on them if they are not protected.

**Melons** such as cantaloupe (also called musk melon) and watermelon are southern delicacies. Honey dew melons are more difficult to grow in our climate, and are rarely successful. Cantaloupes are easily grown in hot summers and they, like watermelons, require large space and plenty of irrigation. Weed control is necessary in the early stages of growth. There are wire cradles to place under your melons as they mature to

> - There is the story of the Japanese melon growers who fitted a box around each immature melon so it would grow square and could be shipped without requiring as much space as a round one. Also, there was a report of giving the watermelons too much fertilizer and when it rained, they exploded. Are these true stories? Maybe!

protect them from rot on the underside. Cantaloupes are sometimes grown on a trellis, but will require some support as they enlarge and ripen. A net hammock can be supplied.

It is easy to know when the cantaloupe is ripe because the fragrance is pronounced and the melon will "slip" from the vine without any tugging. Watermelons are often thumped to test ripeness, and it is an acquired talent. A better test is to look at the underside and if it is slightly yellow and the melon sounds hollow when thumped, it is ripe.

The small watermelons called "ice box" size are much easier to manage and require the same growing conditions but mature earlier. Seedless watermelons are offered in the grocery but they really have very small seeds that are eaten. Animals may raid the patch as melons ripen.

## Peas, Beans and other Legumes

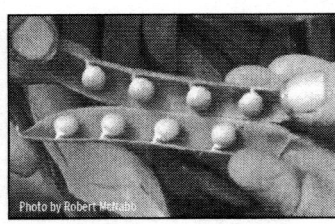

'Green Arrow' English peas

**English peas** are an early spring crop that "goes by" in a few weeks. They are probably the first vegetables you will harvest as they need to be planted when it is still cold. In soil with a pH of 6 or 7, make a trench four inches deep and sow shell peas or edible podded peas (snow peas and sugar snaps) at a spacing of four inches. Cover with an inch of soil. A row of 10 or 12 seeds is enough if you haven't time to freeze them or shell those that require it. The protection of the trench will give the seeds a little warmth on sunny days and in a few weeks, even if it is still very cold, the seeds will finally emerge. As the plants grow taller, gradually fill in the trench until it is level with the surrounding soil. If you have saved a few branches about four or five feet long that you cut off of bushy shrubs, they will be excellent supports to push at least eight inches into the soil beside the young plants. Some varieties claim not to need support, but they get blown about in wind and will be hard to pick if not given a trellis. The tendrils will readily curl around any nearby twig or vine and become a tangle of hard to find peas.

If weeds are numerous, pull carefully as roots of the peas are fragile when young. The white blooms are pollinated by any insect that is out in the early spring and pods grow rapidly. You must not let them stay on the vine even one extra day as they quickly grow too large and coarse to be enjoyed. Fortunately, there are very few insects to damage these early vegetables, and it is okay to succumb to the temptation and eat a few right off of the plants.

**Bush beans and pole beans** are easy to grow and provide welcome fresh vegetables in late May or June. My neighbors always planted "stick" beans because they produce for a long period and are easy to pick. I usually plant bush beans because they produce before the insects get numerous and a short row (about 10 feet long,) that will need harvesting every two or three days will be as much as I want to stoop to pick.

I plant several cultivars on the same day and each requires a different number of days before harvest, so picking will not be in large quantities at any time. If an overabundance occurs, it is not a big task to freeze small amounts. The garden books instruct you to plant a second row of the same variety two weeks later. I have found that the later row finally catches up with the earlier row and suddenly I have an oversupply. If I were planning to can or freeze large quantities, I would sow longer rows. When growing your own, you may pick the pods when slightly immature for a taste treat. Without salt, and cooked for a short period, you will learn that green beans have a truly special flavor. You will never want to eat a canned green bean again!

The **Roma-type of green bean** matures best in cool weather. I have often sowed these in early August for harvest in October. Many times the weather remains cool but no frost occurs until November and several pickings can be enjoyed. These need a trellis as the vines grow four feet tall. It is always a "chance," but gardeners, like gamblers, are always taking chances and sometimes we win and others we lose.

> See **Chapter 5, Gremlins in the Garden** for information about insect control.

Pole beans

**Pole beans** must have tall supports because they grow for a long period. We have used tripods of bamboo, gathered in a neighbor's wild area, and at six feet these were soon overgrown. I think planting in a row and providing a long row of double supports would work best. There are many recent cultivars of pole beans and bush beans and any that do not have "strings" on the pods are going to be best.

**Butterbeans** are usually pole bean types and are very easy to grow. Sowed in May, they thrive even when the weather is hot and dry. If allowed to dry in the pods on the vines at the end of summer, they are shelled for use in soup in winter. We often buy dry beans for this purpose, and the end of harvest ones that dry readily can be used as well as bought ones. It may be necessary to freeze them for a few days to eliminate any trace of larva that may appear while they are in storage.

**Black-eyed peas**, "field peas" or "cow peas" are sowed in May or even in early June. They germinate and grow in extreme drought without supplemental watering. Most are semi-vining and must be planted in rows far apart if you are going to be able to get in to gather them. They do not need fertile soil and, if some humus has been added in recent years, they do not need inoculation with the bacteria that is sold for this purpose. Hungry deer will gobble them up if they are not protected and aphids often suck on the plants. There are many cultivars but purple hull peas are easier to gather when ready because of the color change. A cultivar called 'Top Pick' has pods held above most of the vines. Some have such small peas in the pod, that they are tedious to shell and require many pods to make a few servings.

Black-eyed peas and cornbread pulled farm families through in hard times. They are served, with a bit of "fat back" added for flavor, on New Year's Day to bring good luck in the coming year.

## Peanuts

This interesting crop is sowed in late May. The small Virginia types produce well in our area. Buy peanuts still in the outside shell, but not roasted. Carefully remove the shell but leave the red skin on each nut. Sow several nuts two inches deep and two feet apart in loose soil in a single row or make shorter rows three feet apart. The seeds will germinate in warm soil in a week. Plants will grow two feet tall before the blooms appear. Blooms will be along a stem that will soon hang over the outside of the plant.

After pollination, the "peg," a type of root that grows from these long stems, will bury its tip and there the peanut will form. Plants will keep growing until late summer and you may need to dig a few to see if they are mature. They will be moist and when the crop is mature or frost kills the vines, dig and pull the whole plant up. Allow them to dry in a warm place before pulling off the nuts. Roast them in your oven at 350 degrees for about twenty minutes before eating.

## Okra

**Okra is** the necessary vegetable for a southern garden.

Late April or early May, when the soil has warmed, is the time to soak okra seeds overnight before planting. If the weather is dry, sow the seeds an inch deep and plan to water immediately these seeds that are no longer dormant after being soaked. It may take a week or more for them to emerge, but your faithful attention after six weeks of growth will begin to produce an abundance of pods even from as few as five plants. They should be thinned to two feet apart and, once the dog days of summer arrive, they grow rapidly. After those hollyhock-like blooms open, you will need to begin harvesting every two days to prevent pods from growing too large. Stalks and leaves are irritating to most people, so wear long sleeves and gloves to prevent itching skin. The ideal size is three or four inches unless you plan to slice, coat with corn meal and fry them. If you eat them boiled, add a teaspoon of vinegar to the cooking water to counteract the slime.

Okra in the garden

You will probably have an overabundance of pods and they can be sliced or left whole and frozen without blanching. Slicing seems to produce a better product. By mid-summer, the stalks will be tall and if nothing is done, they continue to grow taller and taller. Look at the main trunk of the plant and make a neat cut just above a bud three feet high. You will be able to pick the pods that result on the side branches without climbing a ladder. Stink bugs sometimes attack small pods late in the season causing them to curl to the side. Remove them as they appear and harvest the good ones for use. Usually there is such an abundance of pods that spraying seems futile. By frost, in fertile soil, the trunk of each plant will be several inches in diameter and require some strength to dig and remove. I have decided to cut them off an inch above the soil and let winter tend to all that remains. If left standing, the birds will enjoy the seeds as the pods break open.

## Onions

In late February, onion sets are abundant. With most things, we choose the biggest, but with onions, the smaller sets are most likely to produce large onions instead of sending up a seed stalk. Sets were grown in the previous season and harvested at this early stage and have been kept dormant through the winter. These can be kept cool for a week or two, but get them planted early. Don't let them begin to sprout in a warm place. Some successful onion growers use small plants instead of sets. These are available in spring in "bunches." They were grown in late fall in cooler climates and look like "green" onions.

Plant them in a trench with just enough soil around them to hold them upright and see if they are more successful than sets in your soil. Space them three inches apart to allow for enlargement of the bulbs. They grow best in the cool weather of spring in a fertile soil with a pH of 6 or 6.5. If your soil contains humus and is well prepared, you may just push each "set" down in the soil until it is just below the surface. Onions need loose fertile soil as they enlarge and also constant moisture. You may want to use some as green onions and these can be planted close together. For green onions, pull some soil around the stems to provide more of the white part to eat. Harvest carefully as needed so you do not disturb the nearby bulbs. Keep weeds from overtaking the plants as they will minimize production. We use short-day types in this area and hope for full size before longer hot days arrive. I have planted seeds in early January in flats in the greenhouse and set them out in late February or early March and, if the thrips were not present, had good luck with the cultivar 'Candy.'

If you have had problems growing large onion bulbs in previous years, they may have been infested with the thrips. This minute insect causes streaks to form on the blades of onion plants and eventually they enter the bulb and cause it to rot. Try to rotate your onions each year to prevent this condition. They are ready to harvest when the tops fall over and should be pulled and allowed to dry before storing or braiding for future use. The famous 'Vidalia' and 'Walla Walla' cultivars are not long keepers. Any that are beginning to spoil may be cleaned, chopped and frozen for later use.

'Egyptian' onions, allium x proliferum, also called "nesting" or "walking" onions are "pass along" plants. A stalk with a cluster of small onions will arise in mid-summer and fall to the soil, take root and may become invasive. Beware! There will always be small onions to use, but be sure you want them before adding them to your garden.

## Peppers

A deer favorite! Yes, they will even eat the leaves of the hot ones.

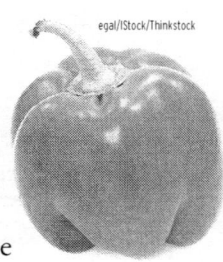

A pepper at its best is one grown in organically enriched soil. Full sun is best, of course, but in extreme heat, it may cause the fruits to blister. A ripe pepper is even better. In past years, we never saw a ripe one and only in recent years has the taste for ripe peppers been cultivated. Many older friends do not even want to taste one of these red or yellow beauties, but they are higher in vitamin C than when green. Small red and yellow sweet peppers have become popular and are called "canape" peppers.

The pepper is a native of the tropics and a perennial. In South Texas, we have seen wild ones growing along alleyways as weeds. Birds eat them and spread the seeds. There, they are called "chilipiquins." The peppers are only one-quarter inch in size, red when ripe, and even though hot, are savored by wildlife. 'Carolina Reaper' is considered to have the highest Scoville rating (pungency) of all. In my greenhouse, I have kept a 'Carolina Reaper' over winter and plan to set it in the garden in late spring. It is producing a few small peppers, but because of the cool temperature, they probably will not be extremely hot. Tabasco peppers were imported from Tabasco, Mexico, and grown by Edmund McIlhenny in Avery Island, Louisiana, in 1868. In processing, they are mashed, salted, fermented, strained and vinegar added before being bottled. You probably have eaten this in Mexican food frequently. The most pungent part of a hot pepper is the tissue that holds the seeds and the flesh is hottest near the stem end. From these beginnings, our large delicious fruits have been developed.

The hot and dry areas of New Mexico are known for their pepper festivals (Hatch, New Mexico, Labor Day weekend). In September and October, there are "ristras" hanging to dry and for sale at every gas station and crossroads. These strings of long hot peppers will dry and keep for months to use in chili and other highly seasoned foods. They are for sale in grocery stores in our area, not as strings, but dried and packaged to keep them dry and preserve the flavor.

Most of us are content to buy our hot pepper seasonings unless we want to make "hot pepper sauce" that was a seasoning for greens in "the old days." It is made by placing ripe hot peppers, usually the long thin ones, in a bottle and covering them with vinegar and allowing it to age for a month before using. It would keep without refrigeration for many months and became more intense as time went by. Always handle hot peppers with gloves and avoid getting the fumes in your nostrils or you will cry.

When growing or buying pepper plants, the experts say look for the stem that slightly turns counter clockwise to get the heaviest-producing plant. This is a feature that we have scarcely noticed. Seeds require warm soil to germinate and bottom heat of 75 degrees is best. Sow them one-quarter inch deep in moderately moist soil and germination will occur in seven or eight days. Seedlings are slow to grow and should be sowed by February 15 in your greenhouse. Window sill light is not strong enough (or warm enough) to produce sturdy seedlings. Peppers prefer a pH of 6.5 to 7, well-drained soil yet frequent watering when bearing fruit. They should be set in the garden when night temperatures are consistently 60 degrees and days 80 degrees. If dry spells occur, they need more water than tomatoes, and frequent watering with a drip system is best. Supplemental feeding will be needed in July to keep them growing well. We once were told to bury a pack of advertising matches under the plant to supply phosphorus, but most of our soils in this area have an abundance of this element and need nitrogen, potassium and magnesium more. As the plants grow, they need support to avoid breaking under heavy loads of fruit, and a tomato cage is suitable. It also will provide a frame to drape a cover of spun bonded polyester or other lightweight fabric over the plant to prevent sunburn of the fruits. Often, when the temperature rises above 90 degrees, peppers will not set fruit. By this time, you probably will have peppers coming along in all stages of growth and if you have chosen the right cultivar, you will be carefully harvesting green peppers to eat.

If you want ripe peppers, you will probably have to wait for a later set of fruits and be patient while watching for fruit worms and other pests until at last they ripen. They may be sliced or chopped and frozen without blanching for later use. Place layers of peppers alternately with plastic film or waxed

> It is interesting to cut open a green pepper and discover a small "second" immature pepper only an inch long inside. Perhaps this is the result of later pollination of the bloom by an insect before it has formed the outer pepper.

paper for easier removal from the freezer container. In late September, the plants put on a large set of blooms, and I have removed many of these to get a lesser number of larger fruits before frost arrives. Even green peppers only two or three inches in diameter can be used and will keep for several weeks in your refrigerator. This is the time to listen to all weather reports and act accordingly as peppers are very tender plants that are killed by even light frost.

## Potatoes

**Sweet potatoes:** Member of the Morning Glory family.

Few of us have space needed to produce sweet potatoes, but those you grow yourself are certainly the best. Small rooted "slips" are for sale in bunches in late spring, but these are usually too many for one garden. Get a friend and share the bunch. Mid to late May is planting time. These are hot weather vegetables. Prepare the soil well, and set the slips deeply, spacing 20 inches apart in the row. Watering will be necessary for two weeks if rain does not come.

When established and signs of growth appear, you will still need to apply one inch of water each week. Most cultivars require 90 to 120 days to mature. A cultivar that produces in 90 days is 'Beauregard.' As the vines spread, they tend to root and only skinny potatoes will develop on these roots. I usually lift the sprawling vines several times to dislodge the forming roots and concentrate the growth on the main stem. They must be dug before frost, but if it catches you unaware, plan to dig the following morning. Use pruners to cut off the vines and start digging 18 inches from the center of the plant, trying not to damage the tender skins. Any that are damaged must be used immediately. Take them, unwashed, to a warm dark place to be cured for two weeks. The skins will become firm and they may be stored in a single layer at 65 degrees for several months.

I have grown my own slips from a purchased sweet potato, but it requires patience and warmth provided by a heat mat under a deep container of damp sand. It is easier to purchase the "slips."

**Irish potatoes**: Solanaceae family.

Natikka/IStock/Thinkstock

This is the potato for cool season growth. It is advisable to purchase seed potatoes that are free of disease. Potatoes are cut in pieces of about one ounce with a minimum of two eyes and allowed to sprout. In loose acid soil (pH of 4.8 to 5.4) that has no fresh manure added (manure causes rot disease), set pieces 4 inches deep and 12 inches apart. As the plants grow, add mulch or "hill up" the soil to keep the forming tubers from being exposed to the sun and turning green and becoming inedible. A feeding of Epsom salts for magnesium and gypsum for calcium will aid growth.

The red 'LaSoda' and 'Norland' cultivars are used as "new" potatoes and some may be "stolen" from the sides of the row when only an inch or two in size. 'Yukon Gold' is the yellow sweet-fleshed small potato that is popular for gourmet tastes.

When digging the large tubers, begin out from the center of the vines two feet and, gradually and carefully, uncover the mature tubers. Store them in a dark place without delay. Any that are injured should be used soon. There is much interest in the yellow cultivars and even the blue ones. These have distinctive flavors and are not commercially available except on rare occasions. All potatoes of these varieties must be stored in a cool dark location to prevent greening. I have seen them left in a cool shady location and sprinkled heavily with lime for storing. They seemed to shrivel, but did not sprout. Their quality

•
**Testing your soil**

Free instructions and mailing containers are available at your county Cooperative Extension Office. There is a $7 charge for the test at the time of this book's printing. It must be paid when you mail your soil sample. If you include your email address, you will get your results quickly.

**Alfa Agricultural Services
961 Donahue Drive
Auburn University
Auburn, AL 36849**

I print this address because often we seal up the box and suddenly realize that we do not have the mailing address.

There is additional information online at www.aces.edu, search soil test.

There is the story of the couple who moved to an old worn out farm seeking to be self-sufficient and sent in a soil sample and asked, "What should we do?" The reply was "Apply for food stamps."

We hope it won't be as bad as that for you, but you will get important information about amending your soil.
•

was not desirable, but this was the way vegetables were stored when ideal conditions were not available.

## Tomatoes

Deer love them!

These are the most popular vegetable grown in home landscapes. They are often placed between shrubs if the resident does not want a large garden. They are even chosen for part of a Square Foot garden. Only a "patio" type could be used in that situation and these also can be planted in large pots that can be moved around on a deck or patio as the angle of the sun changes during summer. Always use purchased potting soil for this and remember that the plant is depending on you to give it water and tend to other needs.

> For tomato ties, you may use narrow strips of cloth. Old sheets or pillow cases make good ties or even the worn out elastic from the waistbands of underwear. The important thing is to let the ties allow some "give" so when the wind blows, the plants are not damaged. Garden string and rolls of tape that are fastened by Velcro are available, but something you are going to discard anyway may be even better. I live away from any convenient shopping area and have to be inventive and use what is available and at hand.

If you have a large vegetable garden, there are many possibilities. You will have to decide if you will cage or stake your tomatoes and if you will grow determinate or indeterminate types. What manner of pruning, if any, will you do and what fertilizer will you use? If you have an established vegetable garden you will need to rotate plantings. Rotation of crops of the solanaceae family is an important aspect. With all of these things in mind, it is wise to make a map of your garden and record each planting location year by year. Tomatoes need a soil that is almost neutral at 6.5 and a soil test will be the best way to determine this.

New cultivars of tomatoes are frequently introduced and even new ideas about growing them. Several years ago, you could buy a "tomato-potato plant" that would give you both vegetables in one plant. This was only possible because both vegetables are of the solanaceae family and a young tomato plant was grafted onto a potato tuber. Another year, it was possible to purchase a tomato grafted on a wild tomato root. This was to provide a more disease resistant and hardier plant. If you have had good luck with an older cultivar, such as 'Better Boy,' then grow it. Try some cherry or plum types. In past years, my first and last tomato of the season has been 'Juliet,' considered a plum, Roma or Italian type.

Green shoulders on fruits are often a problem and no one can point out the exact reason they occur. The writers in northern states blame it on cool weather and that could be a reason in that climate. In our area, they always say it is an "environmental" problem, but never can say exactly what environmental problem is causing this to happen. Some say lack of water, or too much water and others refer to the cultivar. I believe certain cultivars may be prone to this problem. In the cooler weather of fall, I have harvested nice meaty tomatoes without those corky fibers, and from nearby plants there are still the green shoulders and corky fibers. The northern experts say add lots of lime, but here in the south, only add lime if the soil test requires it. In the north, there is more rain and snow and so the soil is probably naturally more acid. I have used fertilizers high in potassium and others high in magnesium and that has made some improvement. We will keep on experimenting with different cultivars and different soil acidity. I plan to add some tomato plants to my flower garden in the coming season and see if that cures the problem if it is one of soil fertility. I will also change to different cultivars, but Park's 'Whopper' has proven a good one for me.

Rotation of crops is especially important with the solanaceae family because all have common insect and disease problems, and our humid climate is conducive to these conditions. Other vegetables of the solanaceae family include peppers, eggplants, potatoes and tomatillos. We are always glad to find new varieties that claim to be resistant to disease. The method you choose of staking or caging and whether you do any sucker removal all affect the outcome. If your garden is in virgin soil that you prepared in the previous fall, you will be successful and not have so many problems, but we seldom can move the whole garden to a new location. A drip irrigation system is advisable and thorough preparation of the soil will have a major effect on the crop.

Growers in our area swear by Black Cow fertilizer as the best. Greensand, a natural mineral containing sand, mined on the coast of New Jersey, contains ample potassium and magnesium needed for strong stems and good fruit production. Use only one-third cup for each plant or four pounds for 100 square feet of garden. Plenty of organic matter in most any form will loosen up clay soil and make sandy soil more moisture retentive. Setting plants deep in the prepared hole will cause more roots to form and give better access to nutrients. Don't forget the collars for cutworm prevention. Hand picking of hornworms can be done early in the morning or late in the evening when they have moved to the top of the plant waiting for the warmth of morning sun. Disease will not be so prevalent if removal of suckers is done and good air circulation is provided by not setting plants too close to each other. Removing diseased leaves may help to some extent but blights are a yearly threat.

Companion planting (this doesn't include weeds) using plants such as dill, that attract pollinators, will insure good fruit set. Some gardeners set plants out early and protect them from cold spells with covers of various kinds, ("wall of water" or even a bucket on cold nights) but this is not a practice advised by the experts. Choosing plants that are sturdy and not yet blooming, and watering when needed, are key factors in getting your plants off to a good start. Of course, mulch is a great help after warm weather has arrived and the plants are well watered. We all look forward to that first tomato of the season and all of the troubles fade away as it is consumed.

## Directional Seed Sowing

Here is a fun idea for kids in spring.

Find a container that is rather tall, five inches across, six or eight inches deep and of clear plastic or at least opaque enough to see through to some extent. Punch several holes in the bottom for drainage and fill it with good potting soil that has been moistened. Use seeds of squash, cucumber or other cucurbit. Have your child plant three seeds near the outside edge of the container about half-inch deep and evenly spaced around the outer edge. One seed should have the point down, another with the point up and a third horizontal. Cover the seeds with a half-inch of soil and water well. Be sure the seeds can be seen from the outside of the container. Place in a light location and watch each day.

If the temperature is about 75 degrees, things should start to happen in a few days. It is interesting to see which seed sends a root down first and emerges from the top of the soil first. You will have to find out by close observation and it will be fun for the whole family. When the plants are growing well and are about three inches tall, it is time to set them in the garden. Water the container well and try to slip out the whole ball of soil and place in the previously prepared hole in the sunniest part of your garden.

The children will have fun watching their plants grow and see which plant blooms and has the first fruit. This would make a good science project.

Many other seeds will germinate faster when "directional planted." Seeds with an eye will send out the radicle (the beginning of a root) first. Remember that word; there is a test at the end of this chapter! If the seed doesn't have to "turn around" to send the radicle into the soil to receive sustenance, it will show green above the soil (seedling leaves). Photosynthesis will take over and the true leaves will appear soon. Try it and see. Cornell University professors have proven this to be true. Look at that okra seed. Even it has a spot on one side where the radicle will sprout. Many seeds are just too small to have an eye that we can see, but that is the way they get their start.

## Drench the Trench

When the soil is dry and it is time to get some seeds planted, take your hoe and make a trench in the soil about three inches deep. Water the soil in this trench thoroughly then add another inch or two of soil, depending on what seeds you are going to sow. Most seeds are planted three times the diameter of the seed. Now water the trench again. Sow the seeds and cover with the dry soil that you had set aside when digging the trench. Firm it down well and water again. If you just wait for rain, ants may steal your seeds, carry them deep into their tunnels and you will never see germination. Remember that the seeds are alive and must be kept constantly moist until growing well. You may be lucky and get some gentle rain which will take care of the garden for a while, but also encourage weed seeds to grow.

When you have an idea of what type of seedling leaves to watch for, and about how long germination requires, it is easier to determine what is the weed and what is the seedling. If you look at your row of seeds each day, you will be successful. Once the plants are growing well, they will have deeper roots and be better able to survive without constant care. You may need to thin out your seedlings in another week, but be sure you have a healthy stand of the desired plant before doing too much thinning.

### Rain, Rain, What a Pain!

It has rained buckets of water for many days.
What is the gardener to do?
Pull weeds!
The petunias have succumbed to rot. The roses suffer black spot!
The gladiola stalks fall in the mud before there is even a bud.
The okra just sits and won't grow.
The tomatoes are splitting and the corn is still low.
What is a gardener to do?
Pull weeds!
Sharpen the hoe, and put it away for a sunny day.
Be glad it's not cotton you are trying to grow.
Listen to the mockingbird's many songs.
Summer will be here before very long.
Clean the mold off the brick walk.
Go visit a neighbor and sit down to talk.
When August comes hot and dry, you will turn the tap
Water will come and you will gratefully sigh.
Remember this water from the sky.
When it's planting season, it's really a pain
But of rain, we should never complain!

— *Mary Lou McNabb, 2013*

# CHAPTER · SEVEN
# Lots of Lists

## DEER-PROOF PLANTS

✓ **Annual flowers**
Ageratum
Cornflower (bachelor button, centaurea cyanus)
Cosmos (sulfur type)
Larkspur
Love in a mist (nigella)
Marigold
Petunia
Poppy
Zinnia
*There may be others but you will have to test them.*

✓ **Herbs** – almost all except parsley and dill
Basil
Borage
Chive – all kinds
French Tarragon
Lavender
Oregano/marjoram
Rosemary
Sage
Thyme

✓ **Perennial flowers/bulbs/corms/tubers**
Chrysanthemum
Coreopsis
Crocus
Daffodil
Dahlia
Hellebore
Hyacinth
Iris (they may eat blooms)
Lily of the Valley
Peony
Salvia
Yarrow

✓ **Shrubs and Vines**
Boxwood
Butterfly bush
Clematis
Holly
Mock Orange
Mountain Laurel
Jasmine
Smoke tree
Snowball viburnum (they try it)
Spirea

## DEER FAVORITES

Small vegetable plants of course are deer and rabbit favorites — nearly all vegetables, except mustard greens and eggplant. Deer will eat many flowers and most vegetation when food is scarce. There are favorite flowers that are much used in landscaping, so consider using something else if deer are prevalent in your area. I have found these to be deer favorites:

| | |
|---|---|
| Camellia | Rose |
| Canna | Snapdragon |
| Daylily | Strawfower |
| Some dianthus | Tulips |
| Hosta | Tomato, pepper, cucumber, greens of most kinds, brassicas of all kinds, and generally everything humans eat. |
| Azalea | |
| Pansy and viola | |
| Phlox, tall garden types | |

## PLANTS THAT WILL NOT THRIVE IN OUR AREA
*Most prefer cold climates.*

| | |
|---|---|
| Rhubarb | Head lettuce |
| Celery | Florence fennel (bulbous type) |
| Delphinium | Lupine |
| Lovage | Late blooming peonies |
| Tulips – use as annuals | |

Biennial flowers such as Canterbury bell (campanula medium) and Foxglove (digitalis) may survive the winter, but not get large enough to bloom by late spring. Both of these plants like cool temperatures in bloom season and we get hot weather too early for their maturity. In some microclimates, they may bloom for a short period before the heat kills them.

# VICIOUS INVASIVES

*Never plant these. Not in alphabetical order, but in avoidance order.*

Equisetum-horse tail rush

Bamboo

Violets – all wild kinds

English ivy – It behaves like kudzu!

Artemisia – any root fragment will grow a new plant. 'Powis Castle' is the only well-behaved perennial artemisia.

Artemisia 'Sweet Annie'– annual artemisia – sheds thousands of seeds

Wisteria

Euphorbia – spurge

Garlic chive

Perilla – relative of basil but a weed

Russian tarragon – not flavorful and the only tarragon grown from seeds, a weed

Morning glory – especially the wild blue type

Cypress vine – ipomoea quamoclit

Clematis – 'Sweet Autumn' clematis, c. paniculata ("silver lace vine")

Comfrey – any root fragment will produce a new plant

Cosmos – yellow-flowered cosmos sulphureus

Sedum acre – 'Creeping Charlie'

Tithonia – tithonia rotundifolia

Four o'clocks – mirabilis jalapa

**Others which are objectionable:**

Egyptian Onion – allium x proliferum

Larkspur

Lantana camara – Most lantanas are annuals. This is the tall pale lavender one.

Horseradish

Butter and eggs – (toad flax) linaria vulgaris. A perennial that spreads by runners and seeds. There are other less aggressive linaria cultivars in white, blue and pink tones that are annuals and not so invasive. Use caution.

Generally beware of gift plants when the giver says "These just grow everywhere in my garden." Most of these are very drought tolerant and will reseed furiously or spread by runners or root pieces regardless of your soil quality.

## JAPANESE BEETLE-PROOF PLANTS

Ageratum
Baby's breath
Begonia
Boxwood
Caladium
Carnation
Celosia
Columbine
Coral Bells
Cornflower
Coreopsis
Daisies
Dusty Miller
Forsythia
Hydrangea
Lady bells – adenophora
Lily
Nigella
Pansy
Poppy
Snapdragon
Strawflower
Sweet William
Veronica

## DROUGHT-PROOF PLANTS

*Most appreciate some water in severe drought.*

### ✓ Annual flowers

Ageratum – houstonianum
Cosmos – sulphureus
Dahlia – tuber
Globe Amaramnth – gomphrena
Lantana
Larkspur
Marigold
Salvia splendens
Vinca – periwinkle
Zinnia

### ✓ Perennials

Achillea – yarrow
Columbine
Coreopsis – thread leaf
Dusty Miller – senecio cineraria
Lantana – 'Miss Huff,' only perennial one
Ornamental onion – allium species
Peony
Salvia farinacea – tender perennial
Salvia officinalis – common garden sage (herb)
Teucrium – germander (herb)
Velvet Sage – salvia leucantha

## PLANT FAMILIES
*Listed as vegetables, herbs and some flowers.*

- **Amaryllis family:** chives, garlic, leek, onion, shallot
- **Crucifer family:** broccoli, Brussels sprout, cabbage, cauliflower, Chinese cabbage, collards, kale, kohlrabi, mustard, radish, rutabaga, turnip, watercress
- **Cucurbit family:** cucumber, gourd, luffa, melons, pumpkin, squash, watermelon
- **Goosefoot family:** beet, spinach, Swiss chard
- **Legume family:** Beans of all kinds, peanut, pea, both English and field peas, soybean
- **Umbellifera family:** anise, caraway, carrot, cilantro-coriander, dill, fennel, parsley
- **Grass family:** corn, oat, rye, wheat
- **Lily family:** asparagus
- **Solanaceae family:** eggplant, pepper, potato, tomato, tomatillo
- **Morning glory family:** sweet potato
- **Compositae family:** All daisy-type flowers, dandelion, endive, lettuce, marigold, sunflower, tansy, yarrow and many others

## THE IMPORTANCE OF CROP ROTATION

Rotation of crops is especially important in the vegetable garden because plants of the same family have common diseases and insects. If planted in the same location year after year, they will continuously have the same problems. Asparagus is considered permanent. Strawberries may be moved in two years. Most of us do not plant corn, potatoes or sweet potatoes. Cover crops of annual rye grass, marigold, greens and legumes are possibilities when we need to plant short-season fillers that we will not harvest but just turn under. Mulch can cover any vacant space and, when turned under, will improve the soil.

As gardeners, we need to recognize names of plant families in order to do crop rotation. A continuing map of your vegetable garden is essential. In spring, we cannot grow the cool season vegetables all season and that means we will change crops at least twice or even three times in each growing season. We plant the cool season ones early and harvest while there is still time to put in a follow up crop to mature before frost. If we are to do complete rotation, we need at least three or four sections of the garden to accomplish this. In other words, crop rotation gets more complicated for us in our long growing season.

A plan of (starting in spring) legumes (English peas), followed by one of the solanaceaes: tomato, pepper, or eggplant, followed by late fall planting of brassicas would be successful in most years. Try especially to rotate the solanaceae vegetables to a different location at every opportunity. Peppers and tomatoes occupy space for a long period. Brassicas are good to follow the solanaceae family because many can be planted late (in fall) to mature in winter and are not heavy feeders. This would be the location for the spring radishes and greens to be followed by cucurbits such as squash and cucumbers that also usually require a long growing season.

If you work out a pattern to follow for three years, the solanaceae family in the third or fourth year can return to the original location. We each will need to work out a pattern that fits our situation and gardening space we have.

## CHAPTER • EIGHT
# Connoisseur's Collection of Cultivars

These choice plants have been in my garden for many years and are seldom seen in the market place. I ordered most and some are difficult to find, but are worth the effort.

### Cyclamen

Cyclamen

The florist cyclamen is usually sold before December holidays and again in spring. It has showy blooms in white, red and shades of pink that face down, but the petals curve upwards (reflex) to become the bloom. It goes dormant after a period of bloom and has been forced for the season as a gift plant.

The hardy cyclamen has heart-shaped leaves in a pattern of dark and light shades of green that arise from the corm in late fall. The flowers are small but are so unexpected in the cold weather that they will charm you. I have observed the perky little blooms in wooded areas in February after a night of 7 degrees. That was 20 years ago when we had severe winters. After a few weeks of blooms, there will be seed pods. They form on a coiled stem that turns down to the soil and are dispensed to germinate near the mother plant. However, ants often carry the seeds away and the young plants will appear in new locations. The tiny seedlings appear in late spring and produce a few small leaves before going dormant.

When dormancy occurs, the corms must be free of any supplemental watering until fall comes. Planting them on a well-drained site makes this possible even in summer rainstorms. Look for the small leaves as they begin to break dormancy in late fall, and carefully transplant them if needed.

Large dormant corms that are flat and about two inches across arrive by mail in fall. It is difficult to tell which side is up. Look carefully for any small evidence of leaves which would indicate the top. The lower side is usually completely clean of any remnants of growth. It is unlikely that the corm will turn itself right side up if you have planted it wrong. They grow best in half shade and on a slope to provide the dry condition that is necessary during dormancy. Cyclamen hederifolium is the hardiest cultivar, but I also have had success with Cyclamen europaeum.

## Heather

Heather is thought of as only a plant for the barrens of Scotland. It is being grown right here in Alabama. I bought my original plant from White Flower Farm in Litchfield, Connecticut. I was living in upper New York State at the time and had just become a Master Gardener there. My friends in the organization asked me to go with them to visit several gardens of people they knew and also to White Flower Farm, which was nearby. We set out early one spring morning on this exciting garden adventure. Each of us had reserved some cash especially for this trip, and we traveled many miles to visit the garden of H. Lincoln (everyone calls him "Linc" and Laura Louise "Timmie") Foster who had written an excellent book entitled "Rock Gardening." This type of garden is very successful in the Northeast because of the alluvial soil, enough moisture at the right time and very cool summers. Their charming, very old Millstream House and garden are located on the edge of a mill stream that once powered grinding stones to turn grain into flour. It has been featured in many magazines and American Rock Garden Society bulletins.

Primroses of many cultivars were in bloom in the back garden and there was scarcely enough space to put your foot anywhere to walk into the garden. I asked for, and was given, permission to walk up the hill and into the garden and was very careful not to step on any valuable plant. I took a photo and my photo is just the same as one I have seen in a "Horticulture" magazine article. We spent an hour there discussing various plants but soon had to leave for Litchfield.

White Flower Farm is an excellent nursery and also sells by catalogue order. It is not named for a family but because the entrance border of perennials is planted with only white flowers. That is where I bought the parent plant of my 'Springwood White' (Erica carnea) heather. I grew it for three years in my New York garden, and when we returned to Alabama, I brought that plant along with several others to my new home.

•
White Flower Farm
www.WhiteFlowerFarm.com
800-503-9624
•

Heather

Here, shown in the photo right, heather is growing on the south side of my garage and thrives with the afternoon shade provided by several large trees that are west of the garage. It is in sandy soil from the foundation of the house and probably not very acid. The catalogue describes this plant as an ideal "weed smotherer" and it has done just that. It grows much taller than the catalogue says, so it is really well situated in this location. The buds begin to form in late fall and when February comes, the show of small white urn-shaped blooms opens. It is a welcome sight in the middle of winter and the protection of the garage helps the blooms to remain attractive on this drought-tolerant plant for over a month. I have tried to interest several nurserymen in selling it, but none have. From just a plant about eight inches across, it has spread by runners that take root to a plant 3 feet across and 24 inches tall. I have never pruned it or tried root cuttings but that is the way it is propagated or by digging rooted runners. These treasures that bloom in unexpected seasons are the occurrences that make gardening so exciting.

## 'Coral Charms' Begonia

While on this same plant-exploring trip, we visited Logee's Greenhouses in Danielson, Connecticut, that was established in 1892. I bought several of their begonias that are a specialty of this nursery. If you have a begonia named 'Coral Charms' or 'Looking Glass,' it most likely came from the plants that I purchased there so many years ago. I have taken numerous begonias to plant swaps and, if you have one of these treasures, that is probably where you acquired it. Logee's has been in business for three or four generations and you may recognize the name Joy Logee Martin as an author of books and magazine articles. Her son, Byron Martin and his wife are the current proprietors of this business. Joy is also a member of The Herb Society of America, and I met her at one of the annual meetings of this organization that I joined over 30 years ago. Logee's catalogue is interesting to people who favor tropical plants and unusual herbs. They sell by mail order. The "old" glass greenhouse was built in 1900 and still contains many of their choice plants. We returned home that evening with a van load of plants and many happy memories of our visit to these gardens and nurseries.

---
•
Logee's Plants for Home & Garden
www.Logees.com
888-330-8038
•
---

## 'Baby's Necklace'

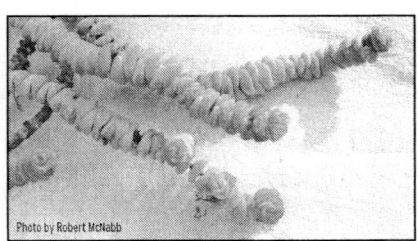
'Baby's Necklace'

While living in Orange County, California, we visited many of their botanical gardens and other places of interest to gardeners. Just north in Los Angeles County, the Huntington Botanical Gardens, Library and Art Gallery in San Marino are of special interest and are near the site of the Rose Parade in Pasadena. Gardeners and art enthusiasts, as well as people who want to spend a day out of doors, will always enjoy a visit here just northeast of Los Angeles. The desert garden contains huge specimens of the world's most rare plants. The library contains many rare books including a Gutenberg Bible and a collection of ancient herbals — including a 1597 copy of John Gerard's "Herball." Roses, camellias, azaleas and fuchsias are featured plants. There were some succulents for sale in the gift shop. I was leaving for Alabama in a few days and decided I could add a plant to my luggage.

> • Huntington Botanical Gardens, Library and Art Gallery
> www.huntington.org
> •

The most interesting plant for sale in the gift shop was a crassula named 'Baby's necklace.' Plant explorations sponsored by the Huntington Garden have introduced many rare plants to the world, and this one was collected in Mexico and introduced by the Huntington in 1975. My visit there was a few years after this plant had been introduced, and I bought this succulent from the gift shop.

I have only shared it with two other people who also are interested in rare succulents. It is a tender crassula and must be grown in part sun in a greenhouse that does not get colder than 40 degrees in winter. It is a series of round "leaves" that are on a central stem and

> • Alabama does not have any regulations about bringing plants into the state, but California does. On one occasion, when entering California, I had to have all of my plants in the car evaluated and approved before they could be brought into the state. The citrus industry is very interested in not introducing harmful insects to their orchards.
> •

look like a necklace. As with all desert plants, it is slow growing and blooms with insignificant small flowers in late spring.

## Banana Shrub

An interesting and somewhat tender plant is the banana shrub. I bought mine in a nursery in Monroe, Louisiana, many years ago. I frequently drove to Monroe while visiting my mother and grandmother in Oak Ridge, Louisiana. I must visit all "plant places" whenever I travel, in search of new plants.

Michelia figo is a member of the magnolia family. It has two-inch cream colored banana smelling blooms in spring for more than a month and grows on the south side of my greenhouse in a very well-drained location. The blooms occasionally set seeds but do not form a large pod like the southern magnolia. The seed, found in the leaf axil where the bloom was produced, has an outer covering that is brown and, when mature, it opens to release the seed. There is an inner covering that is orange and has a hard coat that must be nicked or stratified before it will germinate. Leaves of the banana shrub are three inches long and one inch wide and glossy green. It prefers slightly acid soil and, once established, is drought tolerant. It is evergreen and grows only 10 or possibly 15 feet in height and only six feet wide. If you need a smaller version of the magnolia, this is the plant to choose.

## Arbor Vitae Fern

Arbor vitae fern

A friend in Huntsville gave me a small section of arbor vitae fern several years ago. It has scale-like "fronds" that are similar to the arbor vitae shrub. In severe winters they become reddish, but return to dark green when spring arrives. By producing runners, it has spread to three feet across and grows two feet tall in a half-shade, well-drained location. I planted a small piece of it in my densely shaded deciduous woodland and it has thrived without supplemental water.

I have occasionally used the sprays of leaves in flower arrangements with good keeping qualities. The original plant was handed down through several generations beginning in Cherokee County and later growing near Gadsden in the flower garden of Mrs. Jessie Boyd. She had graduated from the University of Alabama in 1916 and taught school, but made time to develop a three-acre flower garden that was much enjoyed by visitors. As a member of a local garden club, she had entered many flower shows over the years and, at one time, had won more blue ribbons for her flowers than anyone else in Gadsden.

When entering flower shows, the botanical names of plants are required. Mrs. Boyd was able to find the botanical name of the arbor vitae fern – Selaginella pallesenese, a lycopodium – in Liberty Hyde Bailey's "Hortus Third." Lycopods are mosses that evolved from ancient plants that grew in poor soil and never flowered. Small plants of the arbor vitae fern are occasionally offered at the Fern Society sale at the Huntsville Botanical

Garden. An elderly friend who lived near me in Brownsboro grew the "tree fern," also called "spike moss," a lycopod ground cover about five inches tall that also performed best in shade. It was given this common name because the fronds looked like miniature evergreen trees. It is on the endangered plant list and cannot be dug and removed from natural areas.

### 'Christmas Rose'

Another plant that thrives in woodland shade is the hellebore niger, often called 'Christmas Rose.' After blooming, it produces seeds that require double dormancy before germination. This term means that the seed must undergo at least two periods of freezing/thawing temperatures before germination. The blooms are of nodding habit and in shades of cream and off white. The leaves remain most of the year and are on a stalk about six inches tall.

### 'Lenten Rose'

Hellebore orientalis blooms later and is called 'Lenten Rose.' I planted a few many years ago on a wooded slope near a seep of water that provides moisture for this evergreen February and March blooming plant. It has cross pollinated with surrounding plants. After double dormancy, many variations of color have occurred. These plants are not related to roses, but to buttercups (ranunculaceae). Fortunately, deer do not eat either of these.

### Ginger

A third plant in this area of our farm is ginger, Asarum canadense. The "little brown jug" that is the flower forms close to the soil where its seeds can be dispersed to form large clumps. On one of those trips to The Herb Society of America conference, I bought a cultivar that is a hybrid or sport of the wild plant. The leaves are exceptionally large and have cream-colored center veins. It has been there many years and lives among ferns of several kinds that also like the moist area of the seep. Even though these plants are called ginger, they are not culinary plants. Several hardy cyclamen are growing lower on this hillside where, during the wet winter months, all of these plants benefit from moisture. In late summer when the seep above partially dries out, the ferns and ginger survive on limited moisture and the cyclamen receive their period of dormancy.

## Corkscrew Grass

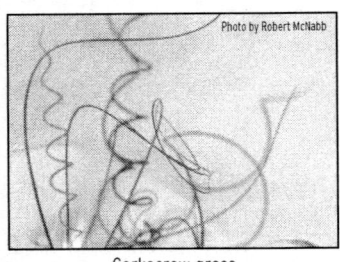

Corkscrew grass

Corkscrew grass is a miniature grass for shade. It grows only four inches tall and has tiny yellow blooms in summer. I bought it on a Master Gardener trip to Athens, Georgia, many years ago. It is really a sedge, but does not have any of the characteristics of the terrible weed called nut sedge. The "leaves" form a swirly corkscrew just as the name suggests. It likes moderate moisture and is so petite that it would be a great addition to any dish garden. It is listed as Cyperaceae caryophylla 'The Beatles' (sedge family) in the Sandy Mush Herb Nursery, Leicester, N.C., handbook. This 80-page handbook is only published every few years, can be downloaded for free, or mailed for a nominal charge. You can learn so much while reading it.

•
Sandy Mush Herb Nursery Handbook
www.sandymushherbs.com
828-683-2014
•

Robert said we only had time for visiting the Vanderbilt mansion (Biltmore) or the herb nursery. You can believe I chose the herb nursery. It was quite an adventure. We had called for directions and carefully followed them as we drove up a one-lane unpaved road with a ravine and creek on the right and dense woodland on the left. Fortunately, there was no other traffic. We were rewarded with an astounding collection of herbs and other interesting plants. I know the Biltmore is an exceptional display of beauty, but I could not miss a chance to visit this nursery.

## 'Tiny Rubies'

•
Bluestone Perennials Inc.
www.bluestoneperennials.com
800-852-5243
•

A second petite plant is **dianthus** 'Tiny Rubies' or Dianthus gratianopolitanus. It was purchased by mail order from Bluestone Perennials Inc. in Madison, Ohio, east of Cleveland near Lake Erie.

This sweet little rose-colored carnation-type flower about three-quarters inch across is only two inches tall when in bloom and forms a cushion of tiny leaves only one inch tall. It seems to be drought proof and no animals have eaten it in the 20 years that I have grown it.

## Alstroemeria Haemantha

Hummingbirds are attracted to red flowers with open throats and the hardy alstroemeria haemantha is a favorite. This is a pass-along plant that I have never seen offered for sale. A hardy hybrid, 'Sweet Laura,' with yellow blooms has been in catalogues for many years.

Alstroemeria Haemantha

Florists use alstroemerias of many colors extensively in winter that are brought from Central American plantings. Hardy alstroemerias grow from roots similar to daylily roots. After blooming, interesting seed pods are formed and scatter seeds nearby. This could be a nuisance in a formal garden, but in less structured areas it is welcomed. Blooms occur on stalks 15 inches tall in early summer and continue until frost. A half-shade protected site is best. Strap-like leaves remain green all winter and tubers several inches below the soil are protected from alternate freezing and thawing. They may be divided in late summer and deep digging will be necessary to get a good cluster of roots. Deer are fond of the alstroemeria.

## Resurrection Fern

If you have several native cedar trees, really juniper, look on the north side of an old one to see if it has a dried up bunch of twisted vegetation. If so, you have found the Resurrection fern. In our humid climate it adopts the grooved trunk of the native cedar to make a home. During dry weather, it shrivels up into just a mass of insignificant dry

Resurrection Fern

vegetation, but when rain returns, it shows a green cluster of fronds. It is very slow growing and seems to have to appear naturally. Windblown spores move it to new locations. I hope you will preserve any that are on your trees.

## Pearlbush

Spring may bring many old friends blooming in the garden — but for a pleasant surprise — plant pearlbush. This wild plant (Exochorda racemosa) is happy with well-drained soil in full or half sun. The native form grows 10 feet tall, but a sport called 'The Bride' attains only four feet in height and may better be suited to a smaller garden. It sends forth tiny pearls of buds in late March that can be brought indoors to enjoy with daffodils and other spring blooming plants. Branches should be cut in the evening and immediately placed in cool water overnight. Those tiny buds eventually open into five petal blooms only an inch across. The spring show is the main attraction on this plant, but any burst of bloom from a shrub that requires no attention even in severe drought, is welcome to a gardener.

## Sternbergia Lutea

Sternbergia lutea is not well known but is a fall blooming bulb. Bulbs are planted in spring or late summer in well-drained soil. Mark the location where you have planted them four inches deep. During hot summer months, they remain dormant and do not require water. As fall rains come, the roots develop and in late September, the yellow crocus-like blooms appear on eight-inch stems. They last several weeks and in large numbers, it is impressive, but a few in a flower garden can also be a pleasant surprise. Deer proof. Order by mail from bulb specialists.

## 'Spring Starflower'

An ideal small bulb for the woodland garden is Ipheion. Commonly called spring starflower, it blooms in late spring on four-inch stems with grass-like foliage. There are blue, pink and white flowered cultivars. They seldom need dividing and will thrive without care once established. Although tiny, these are excellent in the foreground of any half shade garden. Deer proof. Order by mail from bulb specialists.

## 'Red Cascade' Rose

One rose should be in this collection of easy to grow plants. There are many larger flowered ones than 'Red Cascade,' but few are as disease resistant. I have grown it from cuttings taken in early spring and given them to other gardeners. Mine grows just outside my garage door next to a brick wall and, with a southern exposure, blooms even in late fall. Because it has no noticeable fragrance, no insects are attracted to it. I cut it back severely in early spring to get clusters of small blooms for tussie mussies in May (see photo of my tussie mussies in color center spread). There are some thorns, but they are easily stripped off when preparing to use long stems in arrangements. Summer pruning may be done or they may be left to grow tall. In an open location, this plant may grow six feet wide and be considered a shrub rose.

## Abyssinian Gladiola

Acidanthera is marginally hardy in our area, but is an interesting bulb often called Abyssinian gladiola. Bulbs are planted four inches deep in well-drained soil. Failure to live through the winter is usually because of poor drainage or extremely cold weather. The white flowers, with dark maroon centers and foliage, are both similar to those of the gladiola. They are good for cutting when the first blooms are just opening. Bulb specialists offer them for sale and occasionally they are found in packages at the big box stores in spring.

## CHAPTER • NINE
# Heard in the Blueberry Patch

*True tales to tickle and tantalize you.*

We provided a drinking fountain without ice water, a bathroom upstairs in the barn apartment that was vacant, and a picnic table in the shade on the front porch of the barn for customers to rest and relax.

We owned two dogs that were "dropped off" at our farm when they were about six weeks old. They were starved and covered with ticks and fleas. Often, this happened with unwanted dogs before there were animal services in Madison County, Alabama. I knew I must take most of them to the "dog pound," but we did not own a dog when this occurred. These were in dire need of some attention. I took pity on them and, after bathing and feeding them, I decided to keep both of them. They were both females, of course, and obviously sisters.

When they were old enough, I had them spayed. Parentage was mixed, but included some German Shepherd. I named the smaller one, Boots, because her fur was tan and she had white feet and the larger one, Smokey, because her fur was tan with dark streaks. They were happy to make our farm their permanent home and guarded it faithfully.

They became accustomed to having strangers on the premises as we had the blueberry pick-your-own business open every summer. Their summer relief from the heat was to be taken to the basement, and the door always had to be opened to let them go in this cool space under the house. When children came with parents, they always wanted to pet the dogs, and Boots and Smokey were patient for a while. If the children were noisy, it was stressful, and all I had to say was "go to the basement" and they were ahead of me — and on the way to enjoying some peace and quiet.

•

## Country Life

After moving to the country, I was often late. I was accustomed to taking only 15 minutes to drive to most any location in town, but being in a rural area and having to drive several miles to a highway slowed me down. One spring afternoon I was just about ready to make a dash out the front door to be at an appointment. As I glanced out the window to see if my car was still in the shade of a tree, I saw a copperhead snake basking on the top step of the front porch, which faces west. Suddenly, I knew I was going to be late.

I went to the garage and picked up my hoe. I keep the blade well sharpened. Quietly opening the door, I stepped out on the small front porch with hoe in hand, realizing I had no course of retreat. I made one mighty whack right behind the snake's head. He never knew what hit him. No time to clean up the remains. Just step over the snake and be off to the appointment — only five minutes late.

Two 12-year-old boys were heard talking out in the blueberry field while unenthusiastically picking a few berries. "You know, our moms say they want us to have all of these experiences and they bring us along for that reason."

Second boy, "Oh, yeah."

First boy, "I think I have it all figured out. It's really a social occasion for our moms."

"I locked myself out of my car." Well here is the phone and number of the locksmith. He knows the way. He was just here last week to unlock your car.

"How many berries did you eat while you were picking?"

We should weigh the people before and after they go to the field!

We have a "Sin Bin" for donations. "We know, and you know that I know, that you ate lots of berries while out there, so you can just put a little change in this bin and get over your guilt." (This is a great idea, but we never used it.) There were always plenty of berries and we didn't object to customers eating some while they were in the field.

"I called to ask, do you have enough blueberries?" For what, ma'am?

Our oldest customers: A man and wife. He is 92 and she is 89, are brought by their 69-year old daughter. We gave the couple each a chair so they could sit to pick. They had so much fun that they came back the following week.

When leaving in her car, a customer backed into our fence and knocked about twenty feet of it flat. She called her insurance company and they sent out an adjuster to survey the damage and estimate the cost of repair. He made some notes and then got in his car and in leaving, backed into the same fence and knocked down another 10 feet.

If it moves in a hurry, don't worry. (Probably a lizard.) If it moves slow, get a hoe. (Possibly a snake!)

•

## Dogs Know it All

We sometimes go out to work in the garden and stay there for several hours. We leave the garage door open because our tools are stored there, and often we return to get a needed tool. When we go to the garden, our dogs, Boots and Smokey, always go along with us for company. They usually lie down in the grass near our work area and stay with us until our job is finished. Then we all return to the house together. If it is time for them to be fed, they sometimes lead the way back to the house.

On a sunny afternoon in spring, we were returning from the garden and, as I approached the garage, something ran inside. Boots saw it and set out to catch it. She sniffed around some bushel baskets. She was very interested in finding whatever animal I had seen as a brown blur when I came up the driveway. Boots began to bark and use her front feet to move some cardboard boxes and knock over a shovel and rake. She was sure that an animal was in the garage.

Robert arrived on the scene, but said if we would just leave the garage door open the rest of the day, whatever had come in probably would go back out. However, Boots was not content with that idea and began to bark frantically. When Boots gets excited over an animal, she doesn't give up easily. We had to help Boots get that animal! Smokey was a little interested in the chase, but decided to lie down in the grass outside the garage door and let Boots do all of the work.

We started pulling out everything on the back wall of the garage. We really needed to get rid of some of those baskets and boxes anyway. We still couldn't locate the animal, but it was probably really frightened with all of the barking and scrambling around that Boots was doing. The only thing we had not moved was our chest-type freezer. I found a yardstick and poked it under the freezer and out ran a chipmunk. It escaped from Boots and ran out of the garage right in front of Smokey. She grabbed it as it went by and with one chomp of her jaws it was a goner. So we got the garage cleaned out, all because of a chipmunk. We must give Boots credit though, because she insisted that it be done.

•

## The Greatest Compliments

"I wore boots and old clothes because I thought it would be grass and weeds two feet tall, not neatly mowed."

"It is so beautiful and peaceful here."

"This is the neatest farm that I have ever seen. No old car parts or broken down furniture and the grass is all green and mowed. How do just you two do it?" Just plain hard work is the answer.

"Mom, can we come back every day?"

"It's my birthday, and so we do what I like to do, pick blueberries."

"Our library is full of books about intellectuals who retire to a farm and do things similar to this. We thank you for doing this."

Mary Lou, speaking to a doctor, whom she had only ever seen wearing a medical white coat. He came with his wife, shed his shirt while picking and was only wearing shorts and sandals: "Oh, I didn't recognize you without your clothes on!"

•

## Speaking of Clothes

A man who is obviously on his way to the office drives up early on a rainy Friday. It is probably "casual day" for clothing at the office. He is wearing shorts and an old T-shirt. He probably was thinking these thoughts as the following events unfolded: "I'll go out and pick some blueberries while it is cool and then go to the office. There is some fog, but I'm wearing my old clothes, and if I get wet, it doesn't matter. I have my bucket and will get some good ones before most pickers arrive."

He goes to the row we tell him about and says to himself, "Wow, these are really nice berries and it won't take long to get a bucket full."

Time marches on!

"I picked a bucket full in no time and there aren't many other people here."

He pays for his berries and goes to his car thinking, "Well, that didn't cost much, but I've got to get dressed and get to the office. No one seems to be in the vicinity, so I'll just change clothes here at my car."

"First, off with these wet shorts. Glad my undershorts didn't get very wet. Now where did I put those pants to wear to the office? Here I am standing in my shorts and looking for my pants. Oh, there they are, under the 'seat.' (I believe that was a pun.) Well, I've got the right leg on and if I don't kick over my bucket of berries, here goes the left leg. Sure hope no one is looking. Pulled them up and got the zipper zipped. Didn't think I could do it without someone seeing me. Get off this wet T-shirt and dry myself a little. There! Now just get this other T-shirt on — my favorite orange and white striped one. Glad it is casual Friday. Got it on and am off to work. Sure hope no one noticed."

He just thought no one was looking! I happened to be in the kitchen and saw it all! But we will never tell about those boxer shorts with the red hearts printed on them. I'll bet his wife gave them to him for Valentine's Day.

•

## What Shall I Wear to Go Pick Blueberries?

One day, a petite young woman who spoke no English arrived on a hot day, wearing her skintight bicycle shorts, white low-cut blouse and a wide belt. She had makeup on and was beautiful in American "Barbie" clothes. After an hour of picking in the sun, her makeup had melted and run down her face, but we tried not to notice and just hoped she had enjoyed her visit to an American farm.

A young lady from Portugal came with her American friends. She said that she didn't want us to think she was a "city slicker," so she wore her brand new (purchased just for this occasion) overall shorts and red-checked shirt and carried a wicker basket.

"Ah, what shall I wear to go pick those organically grown, unsprayed blueberries? Shorts, of course, since I won't be near any chemicals. I'll just spray my bare legs and arms with lots of this (chemical) insect spray."

## Children are Welcomed! Maybe!

Woman with six wild kids: "Oh, it's like going to the park for entertainment!"

We like to think of it as a business. Our observation, husbands have a calming effect on children, especially boys.

Small boy: "I had a cup of berries, but I put a frog in it and the frog peed on them."

"I'm going to pick some blueberries, dear husband. There are 13 children in the van, some of ours and some of the neighbor's. Well, I'll take all that I can get in the van. So long dear, I'll be back in time for supper." Don't leave any of those kids behind when you go back to town. Count 'em!

Boy about 10 says, "I picked up a toad and it wet on me and my mother says I can't pick blueberries until I wash my hands with soap."

Women who came to pick blueberries: One says to her friend, "I am so frustrated! My computer is down. You know, men and computers are just alike — when they are up and working they are just great, but when they are down, they are worthless!"

I gave them directions to Scott's Apple Orchard, but they found us anyway! Here come the kids from a childcare group on a hot summer day. Oh, oh! Along with the man from the club, who drives, there is one teenage girl in the vanload of humanity that has arrived. Her name is Hannah, and she is a volunteer for a summer that she will never forget!

As soon as the van door is opened, the kids ranging in age from 7 to 12 burst out. (Bad news! The dogs head for the basement!) The kids rush up to the barn and we give each child a small bucket — only there aren't quite enough. We lack one.

"Here, you take a middle-sized bucket," we say. A furor of screaming and grabbing occurs. Everyone now wants a middle-sized bucket. "Okay, now everyone has a middle-sized bucket."

Off to the field! Yelling and name calling and some pushing, shoving and running takes place. Many berries are eaten and kids are running all over the field. Finally, after an hour, that seems like half a day, they decide it is time to quit and go have their berries weighed. Each wants their bucket weighed first, but each must take a turn. They want to press the scale down and see if they can make it register 15 pounds.

"Get your hands off that scale, young'un!" says the driver, who is in charge.

We tell the first child, "Now you have a pound and a half, but we aren't going to sell you the bucket, so we will take off four ounces for it. You have a little over a pound."

Each child has picked about a pound of berries and we put each child's berries in a plastic bag and tie the top closed and decide to charge a dollar for each child. Now, everyone wants a drink of water at the fountain, except one seven-year-old girl, who says, "I want mine in a cup with ice." Robert tells her, "You drink what I drink or go thirsty." Now everyone wants to go to the bathroom. The boys are told, "just go out in the woods." Whew! At last, they are all in the van and headed down the driveway to town. Hannah, you are headed for sainthood! That was a hard way to make $13.00!

Those children, who "explode" from cars and vans, strike terror in the hearts of otherwise brave dogs.

Daycare children from a church are coming. Two teachers, several grandparents and about eight children arrive in two vans. They park in the area of shade under a large tree and get out and come over to the field with their teachers and grandparents. Each child and grandparent has brought a bucket and we send them down to rows where there are lots of ripe berries. The children are well-mannered, talking pleasantly to each other and looking for the largest berry. All pick for about 45 minutes and come up to the barn when the teacher calls them. Each has picked about a pound and we just charge each child one dollar. The grandparents have picked more and pay for theirs separately. All go to the parking area and sit quietly on the railroad ties while waiting to be given a cup of lemonade by the teacher. After all is cleaned up, they calmly climb in the van and drive off to town. Now, that is the way it should be!

## Nature Calls

A young mother who is toilet-training her two-year-old son: "I think you should wash this bucket. I let my boy pee in it and then dumped it under a bush."

A little boy, about six, comes up to the barn checkout counter and asks timidly, "Do you have a bathroom, 'cause I gotta go pee?"

Laurie, our helper for the day, answers, "Yes, upstairs there." So the little boy is off to the bathroom.

An older woman, who has been a customer for many years, is standing nearby and says, "I didn't know you had a bathroom. I always just drop my drawers and pee under a bush."

Laurie, horrified by her confession, says, "You could be arrested for indecent exposure. Please don't ever do that again!"

Now, just where is that extra dark green bush that received the uric acid fertilizer? Well, I guess it wasn't as bad as the man, posing as Superman, but wearing only a cape and eye mask, who ran across the stage at a rock concert. Too bad the Huntsville police were not present that night at the Von Braun Concert Hall.

## Who Comes to Pick Berries?

Retired people, our favorites.

Mamas with kids — entertain the kids.

Thirty-something divorcees looking for berries and perhaps a new romance.

Doctors looking for peace, quiet and time to restore their souls in a peaceful setting.

Our favorite customers: Retired couples who have time to do picking and do it well. Most go out to the field together, but sometimes, the husband, who thinks that berry-picking is woman's work, wants to rest in the shade in front of the barn and shoot the breeze with Robert or anyone else nearby. "I don't pick. My wife does that." They may sit and look at this beautiful valley, but miss all of the fun.

## Tipping is Not Permitted

Often when a customer's bill is several dollars and 75 cents or 80 cents, they tell us to "keep the change." We always insist giving it to them with one of these stories:

Mary Lou: "You will mess up our record keeping with how much we sold. We certainly don't want that to happen."

Robert: "You'd better keep this quarter. You might be stranded in the desert dying of thirst and see a telephone booth off in the distance. You crawl to the booth and discover you can't call for help because you don't have a quarter to put in the slot."

Customer answers, "You'd better keep this quarter, it might be you out in the desert."

•

## Lost and Found

Camera case left hanging in a blueberry bush.

Tupperware containers, not quite a set. They somehow never leave the lids.

"My dinosaur toy!" "My Disney cold cup!" "Our thermos of water!"

Numerous soda cans, gum wrappers, baby bottles, pacifiers, sunglasses and even a gold watch once in a while.

•

## Our Youngest Visitor

The Fourth of July was the next day. A young woman with her four-week-old baby came to gather berries. Other family members were with her. They arrived early and it was a cool day and shady for a few hours in one part of the blueberry field. We sent them there to pick. After a while, the new mother, carrying her baby, came up to the barn to rest while the others continued to pick. Many people admired the dear little baby who responded slightly with a half smile.

Laurie was our helper for the day. She took the baby and said, "Holding this sweet little baby has made my day and whatever happens, I'll remember this and be happy."

This brought smiles from all who were near. The new mother wanted to know how much the baby weighed, so Laurie got a basket and lined it with the baby's blanket and put her in it. The basket was placed on the scale and it read 9 1/2 pounds.

Laurie said, "We must subtract four ounces for the basket. The baby weighs 9 pounds and 4 ounces."

The mother took her baby and replied, "She is gaining nicely."

A man sitting outside the barn heard all that had occurred and said, "I'll give you a dollar a pound for her."

Laurie answered, "This one is already picked and she is worth three dollars a pound." The baby's mother and family, who had just walked up, said they just wouldn't part with their sweet little newborn baby for any price.

### A Bird in the Hand is Worth Three in the Bush!

We discovered a nest of eggs in a bush out in the field and marked the place with yellow flagging tape and told our customers not to pick there because a bird was incubating her eggs. It was a brown thrasher, a rather large shy bird. I watched the nest from a distance and after several days, decided that if I was very quiet and moved slowly, maybe I could gather the berries without disturbing the mother bird. I reached in slowly eight inches from the nest. Suddenly, Mrs. Brown Thrasher hopped off of her nest and gave my hand a hard peck! "Okay, Mrs. Brown Thrasher, you win. This bush is yours for the duration." After a few weeks, we could see the empty nest and took down the flagging tape and resumed picking in the area.

### We Need All of the Help We Can Get

A man who lives down the road a few miles likes to come and bring his five-year-old son, John. His wife is home getting the evening meal ready and is glad to have the five-year-old out from under foot.

John is not interested in picking berries and likes to stay up at the barn and watch all that happens. He pets Boots and Smokey and is not noisy, so they are glad to have attention.

John follows Robert and tries to help by doing what he sees Robert doing. Robert lets him help clean out a few used buckets and stack them neatly for the next customer. John watches as berries are weighed and money collected for the berries. (He catches on quick.) After watching all of this, John shakes out a bag and gives it to a customer to use. (We always shake out each bag to be sure there are no holes where the berries could fall out.) The customer probably thinks John is our grandchild and gives him a half-dollar tip.

At last, his father came up to the barn to pay for the berries he had picked. All was settled and just as they were about to leave, John asked Robert, "Aren't you going to give me a 'tip' for helping?" (John will be a good business man some day!) Of course, his father would not allow that, so John happily went home with just 50 cents for his evening of "work."

•

## Hunger Rules

In the mail occasionally, residents in the Huntsville area get a set of coupons from fast food restaurants for "buy one, get one free." Often these are new menu choices and as economic times are hard, they are frequently used. While waiting in line to order one day, I heard a customer say to his pal, "Well, these sandwiches are usually $3.50 each, but I can get two for $5.00 with this coupon. That is too expensive to feed the extra one to the dog, so I guess I'll let my wife have the extra one."

This brought a chuckle from others waiting in line. We understood how he felt about his wife and the dog! If she heard of this, he probably would be out in the doghouse himself.

•

## Good Neighbor Helps Farmers

One hot summer day in June, I noticed Boots and Smokey doing lots of excited barking out in the edge of the woods away from the barn, but near where we had our "check out" place inside the barn. (You recognize an "alarm" bark from an "attention getting" one if you listen carefully.) Boots is the more aggressive of our dogs and is always seeking out adventure.

I took my hoe, just in case I might need it, and went to see what all of the noise was about. Boots had a rattlesnake cornered under a fallen log on the edge of the woods and it was coiled to strike and gave a warning with that tail of rattles. I don't like to use a hoe to kill a poisonous snake when it knows that I am there, but believe it is best to kill one rather than be surprised by it at a later time.

I remembered that the next door neighbor had a gun and had offered to come and shoot snakes for us, if needed. I shouted for Robert to call him and see if he could come, while I kept watch on the situation. In a few minutes, which seemed like a long time to me, the neighbor arrived with his pistol. He was not alone, however, because he had recently married. His bride and her sister, who happened to be visiting, came over to where I stood guard 20 feet away with the dogs in tow, to observe the event.

About the same time, a customer and her twelve-year-old son came trudging up to the barn to pay for her berries. Her son came over to see what all of the excitement was about. Boys are always fascinated with snakes and he heard us say it was a rattler. The rattler had drawn quite an audience — two dogs, Robert and Mary Lou, neighbor, his bride and her sister, and a customer and her son. Now it was time for action!

Our neighbor drew his pistol and with the first shot hit the rattler in the head. We waited a few minutes before approaching the snake as snakes seem to have a "second life" after the brain is dead when the nervous system still causes it to writhe for a short time. When we were sure the snake was dead, I got a pruner and cut off the rattles and gave them to the boy. He and his mom returned to town with a good story to tell to their friends.

Neighbor, bride and her sister went home satisfied that they had really helped us. A man who had watched the episode from a distance said that he would like to have the snake to skin and mount on his wall. Robert didn't have to bury the victim. Mary Lou was glad to get rid of a poisonous snake and calm returned to MARYMAC Farm.

## Under a Rock or Up in a Tree

All sorts of things happen when we go off to town together and leave the farm in the care of Boots and Smokey. One day, as we returned from a shopping trip, the dogs didn't come to meet us, but remained crouched on either side of some big rocks. A few months earlier, we had hired a man with a backhoe to move these rocks from another location to a driveway across a ravine, and over to the barn where we had our blueberry business office. The largest rock was from a cave formation and one side of it was concave. I had planned to have that side on the top, but when the rock fell out of the bucket of the machine moving it, it fell upside down. I just decided to leave it where it fell, much to the relief of the worker.

The dogs were suspicious that something was under that rock and were going to stay around and see what it was when it emerged. They stayed on guard all day and were still there when we went to bed at ten o'clock.

The following morning when I opened the garage, I immediately knew what was under that rock. Phew! It was a skunk. Boots was an odorous and dejected dog. She had killed the skunk, but paid the price. I was glad it was a warm day, because I knew a tomato juice treatment was in order. I opened a large can of tomato juice, diluted it with water, and was ready to take on a skunked dog. Oh, don't forget the rubber gloves and plastic apron!

Boots came willingly and after a thorough tomato juice rinse, came a real bath in the washtub. Before the sun went down, Boots was her old self, but maybe a little wiser. Robert picked up the dead skunk on a shovel, took it across the field and gave it a proper burial. From that time forward, Boots, especially, and Smokey, too, never showed much interest in skunks.

One Sunday, we returned from church and lunch at a restaurant to find Boots and Smokey on guard below a big tree in our orchard. Robert and

I went inside and changed to our work clothes and returned, bringing a long stick and a hoe, just in case.

Clearly, they had treed a critter. This time it was a brown furry animal, which I did not recognize. It was balanced in the second crotch of branches and hanging on for dear life, just out of reach of human arms holding a long stick. Every time it moved, the dogs jumped and barked with anticipation. They instinctively have the urge to chase and bring down any moving thing, probably even cars and trucks. It is a carryover from their ancestry — those wild dogs of Africa who have no humans to provide their next meal.

I had some books about animals and looked up "groundhog." Sure enough, it said they do, on rare occasions, climb trees. We don't need any groundhogs bent on garden destruction! We decided to have a three-way approach. Robert would use the stick, I would try to shake the tree, and the dogs would "receive" and finish the job. With a few pokes and shakes, the groundhog decided to free-fall and fight it out or make a run for safety. He didn't have a chance!

The moment he landed on the ground, Boots grabbed him and bit him in the neck and it was all over. The dogs seldom eat their prey, and we don't encourage these free meals, so after much praise was bestowed on both dogs, it was time for Robert to get the shovel and head off to the "south forty" and give it a proper burial.

•

## Smokey is Interviewed

It was a Sunday afternoon and a hot summer day and blueberry season had not begun. When we arrived home from church, Boots was excitedly barking at something up in the woods. Smokey was keeping her company, but without the aggressiveness that Boots has always exhibited. I hurried into the house, changed to my work clothes, took my hoe and headed up in the woods to see what Boots had cornered. Just at that time, Smokey suddenly jumped back from an inquisitive sniff and I knew that I was a moment too late. A snake had bitten her. I could see it slither off into the woods between some rocks and noticed those telltale rattles.

Smokey seemed stunned and I realized that she had been bitten on the head just above her eye. It was beginning to swell up already. I led her slowly back to the yard and got her to lie down in the shade. I knew there was no veterinarian available and I would have to be the attending physician. She closed her eyes and I thought she was dead, but she continued to breathe even if it was in short breaths.

I called to Robert to get me some cold wet cloths to lay on her head. I didn't see how she could survive a bite so near the brain, but I stayed with her all afternoon and talked gently to her and kept the cool wet cloths applied to the bite. Her head and neck began to swell and seemed to accumulate fluid.

When evening came, we gently lifted her 60-pound body onto an old bath mat and carried her into the house for the night. When I went to bed, I was sure she would be dead by morning. Several times during the night, I came with a flashlight to see about this dear dog, and even if she couldn't wag her tail or lift her head, she opened her eyes as I spoke to her. I was encouraged that she might live.

I knew that she couldn't eat and that any anti-venom would not help the situation so many hours later, but I called the veterinarian. He told me to come to his office and get a large syringe to force-feed her water. I had Robert go and get the syringe. I forced a little water down her throat as the day went on. She still lay on the rug all that day and we moved her outside in a shady place so if she had to urinate, she would not have the guilt of messing up the house. At night, we carried her inside on the bath mat. The second day, she began to improve and ate a little dog food and began to move about. By the third day, she was greatly improved and ready for the ensuing event.

The TV station was doing a segment on snakes and had called our veterinarian to see what information he could give them on treating pets that had been bitten by a snake. He told them about the anti-venom shot and then mentioned that our dog had been bitten by a rattler but had not received the shot. The TV reporter and his cameraman came to the farm to interview Smokey and me. I told them of the emergency treatment that I had given Smokey and she was able to stand and wag her tail for the interview. When the TV reporter asked how it was to be snake bitten, she had the strength to give her own answer — "Ruff!"

Smokey lived on for many more years and died a natural death. We will never forget these two pets that arrived, uninvited, on our doorstep.

CHAPTER • TEN

# Month by Month in the Garden

Come along with me as we experience a year in the garden at MARYMAC Farm.

The following schedule for planting and tending my garden is what I have used for many years. Weather conditions will have a bearing on what you can accomplish each week and plans may have to be altered. Global warming and climate change will affect planting dates and we will adjust our gardening practices accordingly.

## A Garden Journal

Start a gardening journal if you have not done so in previous years. It will provide valuable information as each season arrives. Always list the year on the cover of your journal and on each page, which should be numbered, and underline seed sowing dates. This is important when the crop is harvested to determine if seeds should be sowed at a different time. When new trees and shrubs are planted, list the cultivar name and location where planted. Labels get lost and details forgotten, so it is best to have a written record of these important facts.

Rotation of crops is essential in the vegetable garden and will be helpful in beds of annual flowers. A map will help in planning this activity. (See **Plant Families** in **Chapter 7, Lots of Lists**.) Record dates of exceptional weather to guide you in what can survive these events. Observe places where water stands and plan to improve the situation, or plant only annuals there. Standing water in winter is death to perennials and even to plants that like wet feet. In winter, the "bare bones" of your garden are visible at this time and you may discover places that need filling in or taking out. Shrubs and trees may need rubbing inside branches removed. Make notes of these things to remind you when pruning and planting seasons arrive.

If deer and rabbits are in your area, get a secure fence erected before plants start growing or you will provide these, and other animals, a feast. It is easier to prepare and prevent than to repair and repent. (See **Chapter 5, Gremlins in the Garden**).

## Removing Unwanted Tree Seedlings

In the shrub border or elsewhere, there may be seedlings of pines and cedars that have appeared. Do not try to pull them, but cut them off at soil level and they will not re-sprout. This must be done at soil level to be effective. If cedars are cut a half-inch higher, the plant will resume growth. Deciduous trees will re-sprout and become even more persistent if cut off at any level. If you are going to dig up small oak seedlings, be sure you get the sprouted acorn, or it will grow another sprout.

When in active growth, scrape the bark of deciduous tree seedlings all the way around the trunk just above the soil level and immediately treat with Round Up or other herbicide. I have made a "swab" from a bamboo stick 10 inches long, with a small piece of cotton enclosed in a covering of cotton fabric. I attached it to the stick with a rubber band. In a small jar with secure lid, I pour a few ounces of undiluted Round Up (Glyphosate) and dip the "swab" in this and apply it to the cut surface. It will require a month or more for the root and above ground parts to die, but eventually the dead top can be broken off and the problem solved. This treatment is most effective in spring and fall when plants are in active growth. It will not be successful after leaves have been shed and the plant is dormant in winter.

## Choosing a Garden Site

If you have a choice, remember that all vegetable and flowering plants, with few exceptions, such as the shade garden, need at least six hours of sun each day. Good drainage, especially in winter, is necessary. A gradual slope is fine, but steep places will need retaining walls of some sort to prevent erosion. Plants and soil will wash out in heavy rain if it is not provided. An abundance of rocks will not provide good rooting conditions. Humus added to clay soil is best. Do not add sand! This will make fine cement. Plants do not grow in cement. If you have sandy soil, add lots of humus each year. It soon decomposes in hot summers and is needed to retain moisture in this type of soil. Large trees nearby have extensive root systems that will rob your garden of moisture and nutrients. If possible, garden away from large trees. Frost pockets are the lowest elevation of a site and the coldest air will settle there at night.

> There used to be a restaurant in Texas that served "compost baked potatoes." It probably was near a stock yard and had access to lots of fresh manure. We hope the potatoes were wrapped in foil and thoroughly cleaned before being served. I am sure this restaurant no longer is in business. The health department probably closed it down!

## ❖ JANUARY ❖

This is a time to read catalogues and learn about new cultivars of many flowers and vegetables. Many plant sources have websites that you can browse for information. Many things are happening on the garden scene. More people are learning to garden and school children are being exposed to nature used as a method of teaching in school gardens. New organic pesticides are being developed and these will help us to be better gardeners with less detrimental effects on our world.

Commercial growers are sowing the new All America Selections knowing that "color sells," so these will be in bloom when ready to be sold. It is really better to purchase a plant that is healthy and in bud, rather than a blooming one for your garden. Let it get roots established in your garden before giving all energy to producing blooms. Outstanding perennial cultivars have been chosen and will be labeled PPA by the Perennial Plant Association. Others will have printed Proven Winners labels and are introduced by this commercial propagator.

Plant fads have come and gone in the past and more will happen in the future. Every spring, some new plant or cultivar of a familiar plant will be introduced. The growers seem to have exclusive rights of propagation for the first year and this is a way to promote new cultivars. Suddenly, "everyone must have the new plant."

Reminisce with me over some from the past. Impatiens: 'New Guinea' coleus: "sun lovers," and many new leaf shapes, Lisianthus: an improved form of eustoma (a wild flower), angelonia, calabrachoa, Dragon Wing begonia, Wave petunia, Wave pansy, 'Diamond Frost' euphorbia, 'Belgian' chrysanthemum, 'Knock Out' rose and 'Encore' azalea. Some have been successful in our climate and others not so.

"Make new friends, but keep the old. Some are silver and the other gold." Let us drink a toast to those that survive and retain their popularity.

If you had a live Christmas tree, save some of the long branches to use as mulch over plants that are in danger of heaving out of the ground during alternate periods of freezing and thawing. If possible in your area, take the remainder to be recycled into chips for mulch.

Prune all grapes on any days that you can work out of doors. If neglected for several years, there will be a tangle of vines that will become diseased and only birds or other wildlife will be able to get any fruit that is produced. (See **Grapes** in **Chapter 2, Small Fruits**.)

Do not work wet soil, but if there is a dry spell, prepare an area of your garden for sowing English peas, snap peas and edible pod peas. (See **Legumes** in **Chapter 6, Variety of Vegetables**.) If any pruning of dead twigs is done, such as on blueberry bushes or deciduous shrubs, save some of these for trellis use for this vine crop.

## In the Greenhouse

The plants that will grow well in your greenhouse depend on the temperature you maintain. Mine is a "cool" greenhouse, 16 by 24 feet in size, and attached to the south side of a barn. It is heated by an electric greenhouse heater using 220 volts, and in summer is cooled by an automatic vent fan. Night temperature is down to 45 degrees before heat turns on, and days get up to 80 degrees before automatic vents open. It has plastic film for a covering and this must be replaced every five or six years. Using a heat mat, I am able to have seedlings germinate quickly and propagate many plants from overwintered mature plants.

Moisten potting soil before use even though the label says otherwise. Use a large plastic bag as a container and moisten only as much soil as you will need for a week or two. You may extend your potting soil by the addition of one-third of Perlite, a white lightweight granular material. When handling this material, be careful not to breathe the dust that is present as it is harmful to your lungs. Using a jug of warm water, pour with one hand while mixing with the other. If the potting soil is to be used immediately, tender seedlings will get off to a good start in the warm soil. The bag of moist soil can be closed to wait for another day. It is convenient to have some ready ahead of time when you want to sow seeds or transplant seedlings on a cloudy day.

Sow lettuce seeds for an indoor crop in March while it is still too cold for planting these out of doors. Late this month, if you are willing to take a chance on the brassicas, sow some seeds. Kohlrabi is one of the most successful for spring. Sudden warm spells after the plants are in the garden may cause the plants to bolt before a harvest can be made, and alternating wet and dry conditions may result in the above-ground kohlrabi "bulbs" splitting.

Broccoli, cabbage and others are best in fall, but some years, we have good luck with a spring crop. If you want to try for that, sow seeds indoors this month. Be sure to label as all seedlings are identical. Make note of this in your journal. Some years we succeed and others, not so.

## Fluorescent Light Gardens

If you do not have a greenhouse, many plants can be grown under fluorescent light. Non-blooming plants do not need a special fluorescent tube, and sturdy seedlings can be produced under fluorescent lighting. A fixture designed to be 16 or 18 inches above the plant shelf can be permanent and the plants grown under it adjusted to the best height for growing. Young seedlings will need to be kept two or three inches from the tubes and larger plants may need to be placed at a greater distance. This can be accommodated by using cardboard boxes of various heights

Mary Lou's under-the-shelf flourescent light garden in the kitchen.

to give each plant the necessary space. Light should be kept on 14 hours each day, and as the plants mature, they will need larger pots. If not started too early, they will be ready when spring arrives, and after hardening off, can be planted in the garden.

Before I had a greenhouse, I grew plants in the kitchen under the fluorescent tubes mounted under my dish shelves. All of this space-robbing plant conglomeration helped my case in asking for a greenhouse.

Many plastic packages from the grocery store can be recycled for greenhouse use. Cakes are sold in large round clear plastic domes and two will make a deep enough container with a clear lid to propagate cuttings. Clear containers make it possible to see when roots appear. Small "forks" that are used to serve hors d'oeuvres are useful when transplanting tiny seedlings. If not available, a vegetable peeler that has a long handle, attached to a slender blade, may be used to lift tiny seedlings. Take the seedling by a leaf and proceed to set it in the new location. (See **Transplanting** under **March** in **Chapter 3, A Year in the Herb Garden.**)

Red plastic jugs in which soap is sold, are good to use as stakes. Wash out the container and use tin snips to cut this bright colored plastic into long pieces to mark special plants. They will be easy to see and last for several years. Write the cultivar information with a permanent marker on the below ground part also, as the top writing may fade, but the below ground information remains longer. It is better to mark dormant perennials and bulbs than to accidentally dig up a root or bulb that you value.

Keep fresh water available for the birds and your feeder filled as the birds have become dependent on this. (We have quit providing food for the birds because of animal problems, but unfrozen water is needed and given each day.)

As the sun's angle changes during winter, some window sill plants may receive too much light and others not enough. Those that like warmth should be moved away from the windows at night, or pull a curtain to protect them from the cold. Poinsettias need to be deprived of excess water as they finish their bloom season. They require specific light and temperature conditions to "bloom" (those colorful parts are really bracts) the following year and if you are not willing to provide this, it is better to just discard them after they begin to shed their leaves. Many other gift plants will begin to fade and most are not worthy of the care required to produce a flowering plant the following year. Enjoy them for the season and then discard when no longer attractive. Pots of hardy bulbs may be kept in a cool location, watered occasionally, until the soil outside is dry enough to give them a place in the garden. Because they are being forced, they probably will not bloom the next year, but will recover in time and be an addition to the spring garden.

The Rieger begonia is a lovely flowering plant and is often given at holidays. It also requires specific conditions to bloom the following year, but would not survive our hot summers. Just enjoy it for the season and dispose of it when no longer attractive.

## ❖ FEBRUARY ❖

The coldest days of the year usually occur during this month.

Get your mail orders placed before some cultivars are sold out. Garden departments are beginning to display seed racks, packaged perennials, spring-planted bulbs and vegetables. Many small packages of seeds are sold at a cheap price. These are usually old cultivars or of poor quality. Buy the best and you will not regret it in the future. When buying those packages of perennials and hardy vegetables, keep them cold until planted. (For best cultivars and planting suggestions, see **Chapter 2, Small Fruits,** and **Chapter 6, Variety of Vegetables**.) Don't leave them in a sun-warmed car while you shop. Keeping them warm will force them to begin growth and they will not be able to survive when set out while it is still cold. They are hardy. As soon as the soil is dry enough and the day mild enough, you should get them in the garden.

Daffodils are blooming and hyacinths are emerging. If a hard freeze is predicted, pick those that are fully open but do not fret about the buds.

Most will survive and bloom later. Check garden perennials to see if they have been heaved out of the soil by alternating periods of freezing and thawing. If so, just gently push them back down. These are the plants that need those Christmas tree branches for insulation.

## Daffodils

Spring is the season to enjoy your fall-planted bulbs. Daffodils, jonquils, and narcissus, or "buttercups" as some southerners call them, are very dependable and long lasting. In spring, driving in rural areas, you will see patches along back roads where we know a house used to stand, as there are clusters of daffodils blooming. Deer and other wildlife do not bother them and they do not require attention after getting established. My grandmother used to sell them from extensive plantings on her farm in North Louisiana and they were about a dollar for a peck. I dug some from the property before it was sold and have grown them for many years in North Alabama.

'King Alfred' Daffodil

There are many newer varieties and improvements over the original 'King Alfred' that was first introduced in 1899. That was the year that the Royal Horticultural Society awarded it their First Class Certificate, their highest award. It was hybridized by John Kendall of Devonshire, but he never saw it bloom as he died before the first bloom occurred. He had spent many years working to introduce a large yellow-cupped bloom that had vigor, true intense yellow color and sturdy stems. Five to seven years are required from seed to first bloom and Mr. Kendall died in 1890. It also had good qualities of fertility and was used as a parent of many successful descendants.

After blooms fade, you may want to remove the seed pods that form, but it isn't absolutely necessary and they will continue to bloom year after year even if this is omitted. You must let the foliage ripen and dry off before removing it. This ensures blooms for the following year. There is a long time when the bulb seems dormant and that is the hot summer. You often plant annuals over the bulb areas for summer color. If you plan to divide or replant to a new location, you must dig daffodils in the next two or three weeks after the foliage dries. We used to believe that the bulbs were dormant all summer, but it seems that they are quietly forming new roots and absorbing energy for the following year after a short dormancy. It is, therefore, best to dig and dry off the bulbs and keep them in a cool (50 to 60 degrees) location such as a basement, until time to replant in late October or early November.

They are best fertilized when planting by working a tablespoon of bone meal into the soil below the bulb. Top application of fertilizer also can be done right after the blooms fade and the foliage is still growing. You can use wood ashes from your fireplace at any season of the year. Remember that animals are attracted to bone meal and will do considerable digging seeking it if they smell it. For this reason, I do not use it here in this rural area.

Daffodils increase rapidly in favorable conditions and when you dig, you will find double and triple bulbs. I usually divide them as they will again reproduce in the next year and soon become crowded. Some of the newer cultivars that claim to be pink or green really do not color well in our hot climate, if planted in the sun. Your preference may be for single or double cultivars, but most any cultivar will do well for you in our climate, if given a reasonable start. If you choose early, mid-season and late blooming cultivars, you may have blooms from late February until early May. Plant drifts of bulbs for the best showing whether you are using daffodils or other spring flowering bulbs. Deer and other mammals enjoy eating many bulbs, but Hooray for Daffodils! No animals eat them.

When you are purchasing any fall-planted bulbs, do not leave them in a sun-heated car while you shop. Overheating will destroy these cool season bulbs. You may plant and give the best of care, but the bulb will never grow if this has happened.

In the greenhouse, look for any insect problems that have developed and take measures to prevent proliferation. On a warm day without wind, tender plants may be moved out of doors for a short period to be sprayed and returned to the greenhouse soon after. Liquid fertilizer, dissolved in warm water, may be applied to plants as they awaken from semi-dormancy in the lengthening days. Vigorous new growth, when half-hard, will provide cuttings in March. Lettuce you sowed in January will be ready to transplant to a larger container for growing indoors, while it is still too cold out of doors for these half hardy plants.

Check stored dahlia tubers and barely moisten any that are shriveled. Too much moisture will result in mold and possible loss. Mid-month, sow peppers and slow growing herbs. If mice have moved in, trap them or they will eat any young plants and even seeds you have sowed in open containers. Do not be in a hurry to sow tomato seeds. They grow rapidly and will get overgrown before time to set them outdoors. Houseplants can be repotted, while there is time, before the spring rush occurs.

> What is a perennial? A plant, that had it lived, would have come back and bloomed for many years!

## Lifespan

A perennial is a long-lived plant propagated from seeds or division. It will bloom for many years, if planted in the right environment and not abused. Some plants considered perennial are short-lived ones. Columbine is one of these and any seeds allowed to fall and grow will not be of the same hybrid because they were pollinated by insects and, lacking a controlled environment, are of mixed parentage.

> In California, where many annuals for production of seeds are grown, fields of certain plants are separated by mountains that prevent insects from cross pollinating the blooms with other colors and forms of specific plants and thus produce seeds true to the hybrid plants. For instance, in one valley, a certain cultivar of a petunia is grown with its partner needed for cross pollination that produces a hybrid. The insects (bees) are not likely to cross the mountain to "mix" the pollen with different petunias grown in a nearby valley. Thus, hybrid plant seeds are produced without pollen being transferred by a human on a greenhouse grown plant.

A biennial is a plant forming a cluster of leaves the first year, lives through a winter, blooms the second year, then dies. (Some live longer.)

An annual is a plant that grows from seed to bloom in one season. If you prevent it from forming seeds, bloom will be prolonged.

A hardy annual is a plant that grows from a seed, usually sowed in the fall, to a small plant in the first year. It can live through a winter in mild climates and blooms in early spring when the weather is cool. After setting seeds, the plant dies.

All plants try to perpetuate their species by forming seeds before dying.

Deadheading of spent blooms will prolong the season of bloom of all flowers and permit perennials to use their energy to form stronger, larger plants for the future.

Late this month, dig a trench and sow English peas in various forms. Be sure to label, as you will need to know if you should pick the immature pods of edible podded peas and snap peas, or wait for the peas to form in their pods for shelling peas. If you planted a patch of mixed greens or set out fall vegetable plants, and winter has not been too severe, mixed greens and kale will be ready for a winter meal and be much appreciated.

On any pleasant day, go to your garden and observe the buds of hellebores and bulbs such as hyacinths and Danford iris. Before the end of this month, if the weather has been kind, they will bloom. Daffodils and early tulips are coming into flower. Roses may be pruned this month or in March.

Prune crape myrtles allowing them to grow in their natural form. Don't perform "crape murder" as is often done on these wonderful plants. This occurs when all trunks are cut off at the same height. Many willowy branches will emerge and make a top heavy plant that may be broken off in severe wind storms.

> Ashes from the fireplace may be scattered around daffodils, lavender and other plants that prefer "sweet" soil. Never use them around acid loving plants such as azaleas, hollies and camellias. Those from the barbeque grill are not usable because of harmful binders that they contain.

Dormant trees and shrubs are planted now and soil prepared for small fruits that will be set out soon.

## ❖ MARCH ❖

Now we can clean up the garden that was left "Messy until March!" List your accomplishments as they occur in your garden journal. Determine what plants you will use to fill in bare places and seek to acquire them. March comes in like a lion, as the song goes and spring is teasing us, but many outdoor garden activities may be accomplished. Refer to notes you made in January or February about pruning of trees and shrubs.

Hydrangeas that bloom on new wood, such as 'Annabelle,' need to be cut down to a height of 14 inches before new growth occurs. Others, many of which are Proven Winners cultivars, bloom on old wood, and should not be pruned until late summer. New ones are frequently introduced and many of these are being used in the Huntsville Botanical Garden. Some new cultivars do not require amendments to the soil to retain their original color. Keep labels and record information in your garden journal. You need to know which hydrangeas to prune in spring and which of the older cultivars require acid or alkaline soil to retain their color. Clematis also have specific pruning needs. Those that bloom on new wood should be pruned severely now and others not until after blooming. If in doubt, prune half of the vine and observe and record in your journal the result. Keep roots cool with mulch and give them a bit of lime to keep the soil alkaline.

If blueberry plants were not pruned last August, now is the time for pruning and fertilizer applications. Weeds are beginning to bloom or have already bloomed and will soon produce seeds. Try to control them, especially in the asparagus row, and continue to fill in the trench on new plantings as growth takes place. Be sure strawberries and other small fruits receive water as needed.

Begin removing dead tops of flowering perennials and herbs that will soon begin growth. Divide and replant the outside sections of fall blooming perennials such as chrysanthemums, 'Goldsturm' rudbeckia, other black-eyed Susans, and gaillardias, but wait to do this for spring blooming perennials until fall. Bypass pruners are best, as pulling on the plants may uproot them. Remove and discard all dead plant material. Wait until new growth appears before removing tops of some late emerging plants, such as velvet sage. Late frosts may damage these marginally hardy plants. Ornamental grasses need the old growth removed before new blades get tall. After pruning, large clumps will look like square bales of hay.

When soil is dry enough, all of the dormant packaged plants need to be set out. Prepare the planting holes with compost and "dig a five dollar hole for even a fifty cent plant" as we used to say. Times have changed, but the same idea applies. Do not set plants deeper than grown in the pot, except for some vegetables. Many potted blooming biennial and perennial plants will tempt you in the market place. (See **Setting Out Plants** under **March** in **Chapter 3, A Year in the Herb Garden**.) Select the budded ones to plant in your garden and keep them watered if you cannot plant immediately.

Work some humus into the soil, set out the plants at the recommended spacing, water well, and then add mulch where needed. It will retain moisture, protect roots from severe heat and cold, and help to control weeds. If over-wintered brassicas are still alive, give them a bit of fertilizer to hasten maturity. It will soon be time to remove them and prepare the soil for vegetables of a different plant family to take their place. (See **Plant Families** list in **Chapter 7, Lots of Lists**.)

Late tulips and other bulbs will put on a colorful show. If the blooms disappear, blame deer. Hyacinths, daffodils, Spanish squill (Hyacinthoides hispanica) and its close relative English bluebell (Hyacinthoides non-scripta), along with grape hyacinths and hellebores are safe and will bloom soon if not blooming now. Iris stalks are rising and will bloom in a month. Set out dahlias that have been kept cool. If dividing seems difficult, prepare a large hole and spread the tubers over a cone of soil. Place a sturdy stake next to the roots before covering with three or four inches of soil. Take care not to injure the central stem that contains the growing tip which must be present for the tuber to sprout.

Vegetable gardening can begin by setting out young brassicas. (See **Brassicas** in **Chapter 6, Variety of Vegetables**.) Place cutworm collars around them and immediately cover these plants with row cover to prevent the need of spraying to control those little green worms. Fill in the trench where the English peas are getting taller. Insert those bare twiggy branches that you saved while pruning, on which the vines will climb. Onion sets and plants are very hardy and should be set in the garden early this month. In loose soil, direct sow carrots (very slow to germinate) and turnips (very quick to germinate). Rocky soil causes misshapen roots. During dry spells, get all tilling done, as a second opportunity may not occur.

Spinach planted last fall will provide good harvests before hot weather arrives. Enjoy these while it is still cool as they quickly go to seed. Rabbits and deer are finishing the winter foliage of many wild plants and will seek the tender new growth of your garden. Even if they did not find it in the first year, without protection, they will soon find it and

> "Thin vegetables quickly or they will grow sickly." This especially applies to radishes, turnips and carrots.

devour all. (See **Chapter 5, Gremlins in the Garden.**)

Red globe-shaped radishes planted in the garden late this month will produce the best of the year, but if sown later, they become strong flavored and pithy. Many new gardeners, young and old, sow the whole package of radish seeds in a small space. Nearly every seed will germinate and soon become crowded. It is hard for us to remove many of those tiny plants that we were so happy to see emerge. Thin them out while they are still small so each has a space of two inches to mature. Water those that remain and harvest when an inch or two in diameter.

Strawberry plants will soon send up bloom stems, but do not need fertilization now. Mulch the plants and get nets ready to use when blooms occur, as the first berries will soon follow. If frost is predicted when there are blooms, pull pine straw over them or temporarily cover with row cover. If removed early the next morning when the sun shines and temperature rises above freezing, the blooms will probably survive and you will have early berries. Fig trees are best pruned in March. Remove dead wood and thin out crowded limbs. Open spaces make harvesting easier when July comes.

Wild flowers are abundant and many public places are open for hikes. If your yard has rocky places and woods, be aware that snakes usually appear about March 15. Learn to recognize the poisonous ones and avoid them.

## In the Greenhouse

Sow strawflowers and statice for dried material to use for crafts. Statice is really a perennial, but will not live over winter in our cold climate. Both of these are slow to grow and need this treatment to be large enough to survive when set in the garden. Petunia seeds are small and the plants are slow growing in their infancy, but if you want double ones, you may have to grow your own. These were once popular but have given way to the single-flowered prolific Wave types and the calibrachoas.

Salvia splendens, formerly only available in red, now has been hybridized to white, pink, and maroon spikes in various heights. It does well in heat and drought and needs six weeks to grow large enough to set out. If you want to get an early start on marigolds and zinnias, sow each seed in a separate pot or cell of a six-pack for planting in the flower garden in empty spaces next month. Let the children sow dwarf marigolds by placing each seed with the dark end down in a cell pack. They are fun to stick in moist soil and germinate in four or five days. In a few weeks, they will be ready to be set in the garden and soon flower.

All young gardeners will enjoy this project and you will observe some new happenings in nature. (See **Directional Seed Sowing** in **Chapter 6, Variety of Vegetables**.)

Now is the time to sow tomatoes. If labeled carefully, one seed in each four-inch pot will not need transplanting and can go into the garden in mid-April. These and other solanaceae are the plants needing rotation every year to prevent continuing diseases. See list of **Plant Families** in **Chapter 7, Lots of Lists** for other plants that may take their place when you give them a new location. Tomato plants with blooms or even small fruits on them are for sale. These, if they will be grown in

---

### A Snake Encounter

One spring day, after considerable rain, it was time to start lawn mowing. We had recently taken our gas cans to the station and had them filled. While Robert was getting the mower out of the barn, I was being helpful and getting a can of gasoline. I opened the door of the small storage shed for gas cans, built on the outside of the barn on a cement pad. I noticed a tiny dark brown tail that disappeared in the little shed, but supposed it was only a lizard. When I opened the shed and pulled out one of the gas cans, there was a rattlesnake, nestled down between two other gas cans.

I shouted to Robert "Snake!" and hurried to the garage to get my hoe. I rushed in and called a neighbor. Luckily one was home. He said he would be over soon to kill the snake. He arrived in a few minutes, so I handed him my hoe and Robert came with a hoe also, which left me weaponless. I grabbed a square-bladed spade that was leaning against the barn and the three of us began to tease that rattler out from behind those gas cans. It all happened so fast, I'm not sure of the details, but the gas cans were pulled out and suddenly the rattler was headed directly towards me! While those two men with their hoes scrambled around, I slammed that square blade of the spade down on the rattler directly behind his head, which was only a few inches from my feet. I made a good thrust and killed him with that one blow. I was trembling and in a cold sweat, but I killed my first rattler and two men were there to back up my story. That is a day I will not forget!

a container all season, may help you get the earliest tomatoes in the neighborhood.

Determinate cultivars, those that grow about four feet tall and produce most of their fruits in a short period, are best for growing in containers. Indeterminate tomatoes continue to grow taller until frost kills them. They may be eight feet tall at the end of the season. Determinate plants will eventually need a five-gallon pot. While the plant is still small, it is easier to transfer it to a large pot. Keep it in the greenhouse until late April. When blossoms occur, gently vibrate the stem each day for pollination. Acquire the necessary cages and stakes now for the outdoor garden. Late this month, sow peat pots of cantaloupes, cucumbers and squash. However, they can be direct sowed in May. Nearly all of the vegetables are heavy feeders, and whether you use liquid, granulated or compost for fertilizer, you need to plan ahead. Try to prepare planting holes in any dry spells and, when there is a cloudy day in April, you will be ready to get them in. Enjoy the last of your lettuce in containers before it goes to seed in a hot greenhouse. Cuttings of tender plants in the greenhouse may be made. If you have a large plant of basil, cuttings are easily rooted in a glass of water on the window sill, but rosemary, scented geraniums and such need more attention and root hormone given. (See **Scented Geraniums** in **Chapter 3, A Year in the Herb Garden**.) Use those clear plastic cake covers for cuttings. You will be able to observe roots as they grow by looking at the bottom of these containers. Kept on a heat mat and shaded and misted frequently, they usually root in two or three weeks. Potted, gradually given more light and hardened off, they will be ready for the garden in late April.

---

•

The hybrid tea rose did not exist until 1867. In that year, Guillot et Fils of France, crossed a hybrid perpetual with a tea rose and the result was the first hybrid large-flowered rose as we know it, named 'La France.' A long line of hybrids has followed with many types of flowers and growth forms. The latest of these were the 'Knock Out' series introduced a few years ago.

•

---

Hybrid tea roses are those that the florist uses and are the most admired of flowers. They have large blooms and are on long stems if pruning has been done correctly. Roses need pruning at this time even if they received some minor pruning last fall. Most are cut to a height of 12 or 14 inches. Always cut just above a bud facing outward as that will cause the bush to be more open and less susceptible to troubles. If there are dead leaves on the soil below plants, remove them. They probably carry the spores of black spot or other diseases. Fertilize and then place fresh mulch beneath the bushes.

> •
> American Rose Society
> www.rose.org
> •

Rust disease has been prevalent on the west coast for several years, but has recently appeared in our area. Fungus causes leaves to have orange spots and fall, but the difference between this and black spot is the color of the shedding leaves. American Rose Society suggests spraying with chemical fungicides, while organic enthusiasts spray with baking soda. Spray programs must begin before the first new growth appears. The important part is to remove all diseased leaves from under the plant and spread fresh mulch. Some cultivars are resistant to the disease and others are killed by it.

## Rose Rosette Disease

Recently in our area, rose rosette disease has appeared. It is believed to be spread by a small mite — visible only by careful examination — that is transferred from one plant to another by wind, human contact or other means. If there are wooded or open areas nearby where wild roses are found, these may be the source of the mites that spread the disease. The indications are thickened stems, excess thorns, crowded leaves that grow in a "rosette shape" and other abnormal patterns of growth.

If you observe your bushes frequently, you would notice unusual shapes and stunted growth of leaves and perhaps think it a result of herbicide drift. If you know no herbicide has been used, you may suspect rose rosette disease. Before removing the bush, consider asking a "Rosarian" friend to look at the condition. There is no known cure and if the disease is confirmed, it is best to remove the plant and as much of the root system as can be dug and discard all of the infected material. It may be a temptation to use some of these extra thorny stems to place around annuals or other plants to discourage cats from digging, but this must not be done. The disease is not believed to be present in the soil where an infected plant was growing, so a new rose could be set in the vacant space.

> Save a few of those thorny stems from healthy plants for placing around other plants in April.

Packaged roses are available and can be planted this month. Most are grafted on to a hardy root and you will see an enlargement at the base of the stem where this was done. Be sure to place the plant so the graft is above the soil level and if shoots should grow from below this graft, remove them. To set out a dormant bush, prepare the soil with humus and make a cone of soil in the hole. Spread the roots over the cone and fill in so the plant is at the same level as when grown in the nursery and with the graft above the soil line. Water well and apply mulch. The rose is said to be America's favorite flower and if given good care it will charm you with the lovely blooms. If only short stems are required when gathering blooms, cut just above a five-leaflet stem for recurring blooms in the near future.

Late this month in the flower garden, sow annuals such as gomphrena and annual periwinkle (catharanthus). They seem to do better when direct sowed. If you once get them established, they will reseed generously although the colors will change due to dominance of one color. Remove seed pods of daffodils and other bulbs. The foliage must be allowed to dry up before being removed. Annuals, set among these drying leaves, will conceal them until you can pull them off to discard. Wild flowers are beginning their best show and you should take some time to see them at the wild flower trail at Huntsville Botanical Garden. Land Trust properties offer guided hikes or just visit nature preserves on your own.

## ❖ APRIL ❖

The most important task is to get the greenhouse empty before the heat of summer. All seedlings need to be in the garden by late April. If grown in peat pots, tear off the top of the pot to get the soil in the pot even with or below the adjacent soil. Peat pots must be moist when plants are set out, otherwise the pot will prevent water from being absorbed by the small plant. I often tear away part of the bottom of the peat pot to be sure the seedling roots will grow in the surrounding soil. Most of our seedlings are single plants and each has its own cell or pot. In commercial greenhouses, several seeds are sowed in each cell to insure that at least one plant will be produced. If there are multiple plants, do not try to divide them. Set out the group and later cut off the smaller ones to allow the more robust one to thrive without competition. Watering for a few weeks will be necessary if rain does not occur.

Only cacti and succulents will tolerate the extreme heat of a sunny greenhouse in summer. I used to hang orchids in trees for the summer, but squirrels, birds and insects took over. Now I arrange shade cloth over these, even the cacti and succulents, and water frequently with a mist nozzle. I plan to clean up the greenhouse and sterilize pots before time to start fall vegetables.

Frost may occur as late as April 15, but many years, the last severe freeze is at the end of March. Keep protective covers handy and listen to weather predictions.

Weeds are still a problem and now the summer ones are germinating. Preen is a weed preventer, but must be used when all weeds are removed and if roots of dandelions and other perennial weeds remain, although all top growth is removed, they will not be eliminated. It now is available with a fertilizer included. Bark mulch products containing Preen are also available. Preen must have the soil loosened so when watered by rain or hose just after application, the soil surface is "sealed" to prevent germination of weed seeds and also all other seeds. After you have set out annuals, this product may be effective in preventing seeds from germinating in beds if applied and watered as directed. If the soil is stirred later, the effect is lost. It is probably most effective when used in public plantings where the mulch will not be disturbed.

Visit your locally owned garden shop and learn about the new organic pesticides and fertilizers that are now available. There are even compost "tea bags" that can be steeped in water to provide organic fertilizer. The big box stores eventually will have these, but customer demand will depend on when that time arrives.

Keep blueberries watered to get the fertilizer that you applied last month dissolved and working, as they will begin blooming later this month. Mulch may need increasing, but this is the only time we place it next to the trunk of a shrub or tree. Don't make "volcanoes" of bark mulch around trees and shrubs, even though you see it done in public places.

The difference is in the mulch material used. By using readily degradable mulch such as decayed leaves, or a porous one such as pine straw, we will not have permanent mulch close to the base of a plant. Perhaps the bark mulch used on public plantings contains Preen to keep it weed free. This protects trees from string trimmer and lawn mower injury. If done in a different setting, heavy mulch of this type would encourage mice to take up residence and chew on tree bark in winter. In these public places, there are, hopefully, no mice because of constant control methods, and the trees will survive.

Remove daffodil seed pods and enjoy all daffodils that bloom this late. Tulips are best treated as annuals in our climate. We do not have cool weather long enough to mature their foliage. Moles eat the bulbs and deer eat the flowers, so this is only a temporary plant for southern gardens. Daylilies are in need of fertilizer for plentiful blooms in June. Ornamental alliums have begun to develop leaves and will also bloom in June. Peony buds are appearing. (See **Peony Pointers** under **May** in this chapter.) Sweet William (Dianthus barbatus) and others such as 'Bath's Pink,' a perennial, are blooming and have a pleasing fragrance. Sweet Williams are biennials that will reseed freely. Columbine is a short lived perennial, so allow seeds to fall for volunteer replacements. Pansies are at their best, but hot weather will take its toll in May. Removing spent flowers and seed pods, although tedious, may help.

Direct seed annuals, such as marigold, celosia, sunflower, gomphrena and zinnia for summer bloom, if you have not started them in pots. Volunteer 'Johnny Jump Up,' vinca, petunia, ageratum, purple robe (nierembergia) and those listed for direct sowing may be plentiful in undisturbed areas. Hardy annuals, those sowed in fall in the wild garden, are making rapid growth and some will have bloomed before March was over. Gather larkspur blooms and seed pods of poppy and nigella for drying. If they will not become a nuisance, let seeds shed for germination in fall and a repeat of these flowers again the following year. They always come up too thick, and thinning will help each remaining plant to perform better. Set out annuals and lay thorny stems that were pruned from roses among them to keep neighborhood cats at bay.

If you set out large potted mums last fall, they may not have survived the winter because the root system did not get well established before winter set in. Chrysanthemums that survived the winter are making new growth. Remove any dead foliage that was not trimmed last month and divide clumps, using the outside parts for new plantings or wait until new growth is tall enough to make cuttings for new plants. If you would like to grow cuttings from overwintered plants, wait until growth is five or six inches tall. These will supply cuttings that will root easily and provide vigorous plants to replace the tired ones from last year. Moving them to a new location will prevent diseases from proliferating. Take stems a few inches tall, remove lower leaves, and dust the cut end with root hormone before inserting into those clear cake containers of moist potting soil. Mist them and keep in a place with indirect light for several weeks. When well rooted, pot them up and gradually expose them to sunlight until they are sturdy enough to set in the garden.

If you would like to try some new cultivars of hardy "cushion" types (those that make mounds of small flowers) or large flowered mums, look online for King's Mums catalogue. As a chrysanthemum judge for many years, it was always exciting to read this catalogue and choose new cultivars to grow and enter in chrysanthemum shows in the fall. Our local chapter of the National Chrysanthemum Society sponsored the national show in Decatur in 1983. Visitors came from as far away as New Zealand. There are shows now on the east and west coasts, but our local chapter has disbanded as have many other chapters. There is an international show in Japan each year. Some of our members attended this show one year and I received many color pictures of the amazing specimens that were on display.

> King's Mums on chrysanthemums
> www.kingsmums.com
>
> National Chrysanthemum Society
> www.mums.org

If you want to grow some of the large-flowered blooms like those that the florist uses, you must grow cultivars that will respond to disbudding. Hardy mums, the cushion types that are found in the market place, will not produce a large bloom even if disbudded. To disbud, means to remove all buds except the terminal one on a stem. Cultivars that respond to disbudding also send out buds at the base and along the stem of the flowering spike. These are carefully removed from the stem as they appear until there is only one bud to form a flower. Other large-flowered mums that are allowed to produce several blooms at the top of the stem are called spray types. Some of these large-flowered early blooming mums have been grown in beds at the Huntsville Botanical Garden. Because nearly all exhibition mums are tender in our climate, small sections of these will be dug and kept in a greenhouse until spring when new plants can be produced.

Sow bush beans and corn in several short rows in early April. If these are killed by a freeze, you will still have an opportunity for a second sowing later in this month or in May. Potatoes are pushing up foliage and a little frost may damage the tops, but they will survive. Continue to add soil or heavy mulch so the young tubers will not be exposed to light and become green and inedible. Tomatoes can be set in well-prepared holes and need their cages for protection from deer, even when young. They are especially tender and must be protected when frost is threatened. Late this month, the peppers and eggplants will be ready for setting out. Harvest asparagus tips of those that are well established and enjoy this treat from the spring garden.

Shade gardens are beginning to become showy with hostas, ferns, and others. Tender started plants of caladium can be set out late this month when the soil has warmed. I have a clump of primroses that continues to thrive although these plants are primarily for cold climates. It was purchased many years ago and has red blooms with a yellow edge. I enjoyed the many colorful primroses in the Seattle area and in the northeast, where we lived in past years, and decided to give them a try here. Only this one plant has survived. Lily of the valley (Convallaria majalis) will produce its fragrant blooms soon. Epimediums are spreading low-growing perennials that bloom later in yellow or white columbine-type flowers. They and many wild flowers thrive in deciduous shade. Calla lily and the rain lily (zephranthes, related to the atamasco lily) bloom in moist shade. Coleus and wax begonias, the dwarf fibrous rooted ones, add color in the shade garden.

Azaleas will be at their best. I have seen the 'Encore' azaleas at the Huntsville Botanical Garden in late August and decided they are valuable for fall color. They do not seem as hardy and vigorous as our spring blooming Indica and Kurume cultivars, but with care, put on a colorful show in spring and again in fall.

Hardy potted azaleas purchased in bloom need special care in setting in the garden. The root ball must be loosened and roots that have encircled the inside of the pot must be spread out and encouraged to grow into the surrounding soil. Many a dead azalea has been pulled out of a planting hole with all roots just as they were in the nursery can. Water did not penetrate the soil ball and the plant perished for lack of water. Provide for the eventual size of these landscape treasures and give fertilizer after bloom season is complete. Prune overgrown specimens after blooms fade but before July 4. When allowed to keep their natural form, they are pleasing additions to the landscape.

Late April is the time to visit perennial gardens. Irises are at their best and many other less showy flowers are in their initial burst of bloom for the year. New color combinations of iris blooms with frilly edges continue to entice the enthusiast to acquire the latest innovations. There are early, mid-season and late cultivars and rebloomers flowering again in late summer. Dwarfs and those with variegated leaves also add interest to the garden after blooms have gone by.

Larkspur

Velvet sage, a tender perennial, may have survived the winter and is just beginning to show signs of growth. This is the time to remove the dead bloom stalks of last fall and transplant outer parts to new locations. If nothing is showing yet, wait a few more weeks. Cut back perennial asters to 10 inches and divide any that crowd out their neighbors. Hydrangea 'Annabelle' also benefits from severe pruning at this time. Plant the gladiola corms in a place where their foliage will not be apparent after the bloom season. Gather blooms of larkspur and cornflower and seed pods of nigella and poppy for drying. The colors will be more intense while it is cool.

> Look for the "bunny rabbit" head in a larkspur bloom. If you view it from the side you will notice a collar of petals around the bunny's head, two tiny "ears" and the face in profile.

## Drying Flowers for Winter Decoration

There have been many books and articles written about drying flowers, and I will add just a few more words on the subject. Many of the flowers used are almost wildlings. They are often sowed in out of the way places on your property in the fall to sprout in cool weather, live through winter and bloom in early or late spring and then die (hardy annuals). Those needing this treatment include 'Shirley' poppy and other poppies, larkspur, 'Love in a Mist' (nigella), mainly grown for the attractive seed pods, and bachelor button, also called cornflower (centaurea). Remember that they are nearly wildlings and you may never get rid of them if sown in your flower garden. Most of these are dried by hanging upside down in a dry and dark location.

One of the best of the summer growing ones is the strawflower. There are tall ones and dwarf ones. It is seldom found for sale as a bedding plant, but is one of the best for drying and will keep its color and shape for as long as five years. Find a package of seeds on the seed rack in spring and grow some. They are fairly easy to grow in the garden or in the greenhouse as individual plants to be set out after danger of frost, spacing them 12 to 14 inches apart. In rich soil, they will grow four feet tall and need to be staked. By frequent picking of the blooms, they will keep producing until frost. The dwarf cultivars grow only two feet tall and do not need staking. The colors are yellows, pinks and brighter reds and sometimes white, and blooms are usually about two or three inches across. The secrets of drying them are to pick when the bloom is only half open as it will open further as it dries. If you do not have long stems and are going to use them in a situation requiring long stems, immediately after picking cut the stem just under the blossom and insert a lightweight florist wire. Stand them in a dark location and, as they dry, the bloom will open more and adhere firmly to the wire stem. If it is necessary to wait a few hours after picking, the base of the bloom will have hardened and you cannot insert the wire. When there are long stems to pick, just strip off all leaves. Then bunch a few stems together and put a rubber band around them with string through the rubber band and hang them upside down to dry. They will dry in a week and keep their color very well for many years.

Another flower that is excellent for drying is celosia or cockscomb. There are two forms and the crested one in tones of red and pink is probably best for drying. Yellow tones seem to brown out when dried. There are plume types also and they too are good dried, but again only in the red and pink tones. They grow easily from seeds sown in the garden, but are eaten by deer. On occasion, the stems of this flower become wide or striated, but that only enhances their appeal. You will need to remove any seeds formed just below the crested bloom as they shed easily and scatter under the arrangement.

## ❖ MAY ❖

Gilbert and Sullivan wrote about "the flowers that bloom in May, tra-la." The biennials and perennials are doing just that. The hardy annuals are finishing their display and will be pulled out soon. Peonies in all their glory bloom this month, although early ones often have blooms in April. Peony blooms may be dried for later use, but with great amounts of moisture in them, the silica gel method is best.

> Ants that are on the peony buds are only seeking the nectar that buds exude, not opening the blooms as has been a part of folklore for centuries.

### Peony Pointers

The peony is one of my favorite plants and I have grown them for many years. I ordered several roots from a mail order nursery in 1981 and also have had some given to me that were handed down from great-grandparents' gardens in Michigan. Many other peony enthusiasts also report this ancestral event. Of course, these handed-down roots are the progeny of the original plant. But the family connection is important to us as we honor the memory of family members we did not ever meet. If you have one of these doubles that has red flecks on a few of the white petals, it is probably 'Festiva Maxima' that was introduced in 1851 and was brought to the new world by the early settlers. Our ancestors in the northern part of the country grew the fern leaf peony (P. tenufolia) but, requiring much colder temperature, it is not suitable for the south.

There are many breeders of peonies in the northern states, where these plants, originally found in the Orient, thrive. Catalogues with pictures will convince you to order some. Cultivars with various kinds of blooms are available to please any gardener. Due to our short period of cool spring weather, choose only early and mid-season cultivars. A sunny well-drained location is necessary, but afternoon shade will enhance flower color and permit mid-season types to perform best. Double blooms often get heavy with rain and tend to flop. Semi-double and single blooms hold up fairly well in rains, but staking may be mandatory for good display. I have used cut off tomato cages placed when the plants were set out and these remain in the garden year around. This makes it difficult to trim off dead foliage in fall, but makes life a little less complicated in spring, when so many other plants demand attention.

Roots are usually shipped in late fall and need to be planted soon after arrival. They are most often a clump of cut off roots that have no tiny feeder roots, but have three "eyes." Be careful not to injure these small growing tips as the root will not grow a top without them. (More on this later.) Space them three or four feet apart in an open space. If planted near trees or large shrubs, they will soon outgrow the space and also be bothered with disease from lack of air circulation. Peonies grow from three to four feet tall. Amend the soil with humus and bone meal for this long-lived plant as it resents transplanting. The eyes (growing tips) of the root should be placed at soil level or just an inch below. If planted too deep, no blooms will occur. Fill in the hole after setting the root on a cone of soil. Water and wait. It may require two or three years before the plant is growing well enough to produce much bloom. It prefers pH of 6.5 to 7, so wood ashes may be sprinkled around the crown. Cultivation to prevent weed competition must be accomplished until the plant has had time to get established. After a few years, fertilizer such as 13-13-13 may be used in early spring. It should be applied at the outside of the plant as you may injure emerging eyes if you cultivate near the crown.

If diseases become a problem, spray with a fungicide as soon as the eyes emerge and again as the foliage develops and, finally, just before the buds begin to open. Botrytis is the principal disease and fungicides such as those used for rose black spot are effective. Thrips are often hiding in double blooms and need to be eradicated. Remove faded blooms and seed pods as they appear. Seedlings are not going to be of worth and seed production uses energy needed for the following year. I have one seedling in my garden and it blooms before all others, but is only a curiosity.

Leaf spot diseases also may develop late in the season. Cut off at soil level all top growth after it has blackened from frost or when the plant goes dormant in late summer. Remove from the garden and destroy it.

To produce one large bloom, remove all side buds that grow on the main stem. To strengthen the plant, leave as much foliage as possible when picking blooms. When they are just beginning to open, cut flowers with a sharp pruner or knife and plunge into deep water for several hours before displaying. If flowers are going to be needed at a later date, they may be cut when the first petals are beginning to unfurl and refrigerated for many days. Florists sometimes refrigerate buds for four weeks to have them when needed. They will be brought to a warmer area a day before use to allow the petals to fully open.

We have been led to believe that the eye of the root must be present for the plant to produce foliage and subsequent bloom. This is true for most peonies, but there are a few exceptions to this statement. A single white peony cultivar, 'Prairie Moon,' has demonstrated in my garden that the eye is not needed for this cultivar. I have dug and transplanted several roots of this cultivar and had top growth of a new plant reappear several years later in the same place where the original one was removed. This was first recorded in 1562 and again in 1907 and as late as 1976. It is believed to be influenced by genetic content. One breeder is experimenting with this "freak" of nature and more new peonies may be developed in the future with this characteristic.

> Auburn University is experimenting with peony cultivars that will grow in the southern part of our state, but peonies are usually recommended for cooler regions.

The tree peony has larger blooms and the only true yellow flowers in the peony family. It is a shrub eventually growing six feet tall and wide. Only dead leaves are removed and no pruning of stems is done. When planting, the graft, which is on an herbaceous (top growth dies off in winter) peony root, should be placed below the soil line so the scion (upper part) of the plant will eventually develop roots of its own. There is an impressive collection of tree peonies at the Huntsville Botanical Garden. They bloom a few weeks later than the herbaceous ones.

## A Garden of Blue Flowers

If you desire something different from multicolor beds of flowers, plant only blue ones. There is not an abundance of blue flowers, but a mixture of perennials, biennials, annuals and bulbs can make this possible if much advance planning is done. Gray or silver foliage will enhance the effect. This could be done in a deep bed facing south or in an open area to be viewed from all sides. The following suggestions are for a sunny site. Early spring blooms provided by pansies and violas, with blue hyacinths planted among them, must be planned in fall. Cornflower (bachelor button) and tall blue larkspur seeded in the far background in fall will bloom along with them in May, but soon be over and must be pulled out before scattering seeds. Gladiolas in lavender shades may follow for the background, but also bloom for a short time. The tallest background plant could be velvet sage (Salvia leucantha.) This will be the last to bloom in September and October. Aster frikartii, almost a shrub, blooms just before the velvet sage. Just in front of it, plant perovskia (Russian sage) that will bloom in July and until frost and also has silver foliage. Not showy, but with gray foliage, use the herb lavender, and in front of it set out salvia farinacea 'Victoria.' The dark blue blooms of salvia guaranitica 'Black and Blue' are sparse, but also of intermediate height. Perennials such as these will remain for many years and the annuals such as ageratum (many heights) and scabiosa, sometimes perennial, can be used in the foreground and varied from year to year. The annual nierembergia 'Purple Robe' produces cup-shaped up-facing blooms on six-inch plants all summer regardless of weather. It is seldom offered as a bedding plant, but direct sowing will succeed. Occasionally, the flower reverts to white. Experimentation will be an interesting ongoing project and recording your successes will be helpful. These suggestions are blue-flowered plants that I have grown in my garden and most are dependable.

Tomatoes and all other vegetables will appreciate mulch when heat and dry spells occur. Cucumbers need help getting their tendrils started on the trellis. Once they start climbing, they may not need much more encouragement and will produce straight fruits. Vegetables such as corn and okra can be sowed in the vegetable garden early this month. Winter squash, only labeled as "winter" because it can be stored and eaten all winter, requires much space. Butternut and spaghetti squash grow well in our heat and a few other winter types have been successfully produced in the Demonstration Vegetable Garden at the Huntsville Botanical Garden, but they are a staple of the cooler gardens of the northeast. Allow adequate space for these spreaders. Mid-May is fine for planting heat lovers such as sweet potato slips and black eyed peas of all types. (See **Sweet Potatoes** and **Legumes** in **Chapter 6, Variety of Vegetables**.) These thrive without attention and the only pests besides deer, are aphids.

Strawberries are about over but runners are crowding the patch. You may insert pots of soil under the runners closest to the original plants and these will root and be ready to set out in a month. If there is no rain, you will need to water these pots to keep their developing roots moist. Mulch paths using layers of newspaper or cardboard covered with wood chips. As much as possible, avoid spreading weed seeds by tracking them in on paths as you tend the plants. Irises are at their best and need water until dormancy occurs after bloom. Remove seed pods on these and peonies. Most perennials except irises will benefit from mulch applied after a rain. It will moderate soil temperature during the heat of summer and keep soil moist in dry spells. Make compost of grass clippings and disease-free garden residue along with any leaves that are still bagged from last fall. Bury kitchen fruit and vegetable trimmings in the compost bin. I hesitate to bury seeds of tomatoes, squash, peppers and others that insist on sprouting. Any of these that grow will not be true to the parent if it was a hybrid. Frequent turning will keep them uprooted.

> In the heat of summer, I talked to my plants, but none replied. So I sang to my plants. Then they all died!

## ❖ JUNE ❖

A month of harvest and appreciation of all that you have accomplished. Welcome visitors. Record events in your journal. Daylilies (hemerocallis) are at their best in public plantings. If this is a special interest to you, visit the collection of 800 cultivars at the Daylily Garden at the Huntsville Botanical Garden that will be blooming all of June and some even in July. Each year, after the bloom season is over, many are dug and potted to be sold in September at the annual Daylily Garden sale at the Huntsville Botanical Garden.

These plants are among the most satisfying plants in the perennial garden. When clumps have become very large, they may be dug and divided by placing two garden forks back to back down in the clump and prying them apart. Each resulting section may again be divided and these divisions are potted or reset in the garden. Roots are spread over a cone of soil and no deeper than previously growing. Some are completely dormant in winter and others retain some foliage year round. Hybrids have produced blooms of all forms and colors, with the exception of blue and pure white. They have come a long way from the original "ditch" lily (H. fulva) and deer relish all of them.

There are also outstanding collections of hostas, ferns, wildflowers and native azaleas. Ask about other local plant societies that feature informative programs on each of these plants. Lilies, ornamental alliums, lavender, and culinary sage are in bloom. Gather lavender, sage and hydrangea blooms for drying and craft use in winter. Tip pinch blooming stems of coleus and basil for bushy plants. Annuals, that are the basic show of color during the middle of summer, may need dead heading. Water during dry spells. Chrysanthemum plants that have formed "premature" buds and are getting tall should be cut back to six inches by July 4, and that day is coming soon. Prune azaleas that are getting too large. Roses are plentiful if spraying, fertilizing and removing spent blooms have been accomplished.

Yes, it is hot, but dedicated gardeners go to their gardens early or late in the day.

Vegetable gardens, if watered faithfully during dry spells, are growing vigorously. Provide a water supply near your garden for the birds. They need a drink and may start pecking tomatoes because they are thirsty. English peas are finished. Pull them out and bury the vines. Sow dill or other crops that attract pollinators in their place. This row may be where you will set out the fall vegetables or sow greens when September arrives. It is time to allow the asparagus to grow ferns to strengthen the plants for next spring. Radishes grown in the heat will be too strong flavored but the peppers that will soon be large enough for use appreciate the heat. Broccoli, spinach and other cool season crops are bolting to seed and must be removed to make space for later crops. Till or turn the soil, working in the old mulch. Store all row covers for reuse in fall. Dig potatoes and store in a dark cool location. Small-to-medium-size cultivars of pumpkins may be sowed but need space to spread. Sow field peas in any vacant space. Plan to turn under later or leave to mature and harvest as dry shelled peas for winter soup. It is a temptation to abandon the garden to a crop of weeds, but persist. The best may be yet to come.

Use compost or a low nitrogen fertilizer to sidedress tomatoes. If given an oversupply of nitrogen, the plants will grow more leaves than fruits. A steady supply of water is needed to prevent the fruits from splitting when heavy rains occur. If blight is likely, start a spray program using one of the new organic compounds that are available or a tablespoon of baking soda mixed in one gallon of water. Gather cucumbers and summer squash while they are small. Cantaloupes are enlarging and placing a support under each will prevent moisture and insects in the soil from damaging them. A pot turned upside down or some other object can be used. When ripe, they separate from the stem with just a slight pull. In mid-month, pick the first blueberries of the season, but taste to be sure they are really ripe. The heaviest production will occur in July.

## ❖ JULY ❖

Are your flowers and other features of the landscape near enough to the windows to be observed from indoors? This makes them more enjoyable in extreme temperatures of summer and winter. That is what "picture windows" are all about! Spend the early and late hours of the day grooming plants and observing nature. Maybe there are bats in your neighborhood that live in wooded areas or caves. Their pattern of flight is different from birds and they are interesting to observe at dusk as they seek food. Lantana creeps across the garden path while blooms continue to attract butterflies. Agastache

> The only thing you can grow in the shade is older! Sounds good about now! But, of course, moss, weeds and ivy grow in dense shade quite well.

(hyssop) will entice hummingbirds with their lavender bloom spikes and some cultivars have lime green foliage. Boltonia 'Snowbank' gives us airy white blooms for bouquets. Flower heads of sedum 'Autumn Joy' are beginning to enlarge for their show from August until winter. Annuals have become tired and need some refreshing with fertilizer and water. Pentas are luring butterflies and periwinkles are at the height of bloom. Annual gomphrena continues to bloom through drought along with the nearly perennial orange one, 'Strawberry Fields'. Both are excellent dried flowers. Deadhead the marigolds or teach a grandchild how much fun it is to snap them off. Sow dwarf zinnias for fall bloom that will be less troubled by mildew.

July is the time to go swimming and eat watermelon. At weekly markets, okra, melon, cucumber, tomato and other hot season vegetables are plentiful and in your garden that is also happening. Gather okra every two days. If the plants are getting too tall, cut half of your plants off at a height of three or four feet. The remaining stalk of these pruned plants will send out branches and pods that can be picked easily, while you still harvest those from the tall plants that were not cut back. Onions are nearly ready and fertilizer and water will encourage large bulbs. When tops fall over, they are ready to be harvested and allowed to dry for a week before storing in a cool location. If they are plentiful, chop and freeze some for later use. Dig garlic and place in a shady location to dry. Set aside a few cloves to be separated and replanted in October. The Egyptian onions, also called "nesting" or "walking" onions are sending out clusters of small bulbs and, if you gather them, it will prevent them taking over your garden. These are true "pass along" plants. Beware!

Hill up corn rows, apply some nitrogen fertilizer, then add mulch. Apply oil spray, or Neem dust or spray, to silks for prevention of corn earworms. These insect larvae also attack peppers and tomatoes while they are green, so spray fruits in all stages of growth. Always pick peppers by cutting off with a pruner. Plants are very brittle and, when heavy with developing fruit, break easily. As tomatoes ripen, you may need to give some shade to avoid "sunburned" fruits. Use clothes pins to fasten covers of brown paper or newspaper over the cages to prevent this situation. If you have more than can be used fresh, they can be "stewed" for 20 minutes and frozen in containers for use in winter. Canning takes more time, but many people do it. Just be sure to follow directions for boiling water bath processing. There is no easy way to accomplish a safe product without proper preparation.

Cucumbers need to be harvested every two days and even then, some will be hidden and escape your attention until too large. Keep these picked and discard them to encourage the plant to continue producing. Pickles are easy with spice mixes provided by Mrs. Wages, but also require proper preserving methods. Jams and jellies are much appreciated in winter. The frozen ones are acceptable, but we really want the taste of those Grandma made. Using packaged pectin hastens the process and there are pectins that require less sugar than the standard ones. Local peaches are ripening. Those in the grocery store have been picked hard and green to survive shipping and may never develop sweetness. Bunch grapes and blackberries will be ready for harvest at this time. Pick blueberries to freeze. They have health benefits and are easy to prepare for freezing. (See **Recipes** and other information in **Chapter 1, Blueberry Cultivation**.)

The greenhouse is too hot to produce sturdy transplants of brassicas, but the fluorescent garden in your cool house will provide the right conditions in mid-July to get these plants started and ready to set out later.

> •
> Kipling commented, "Beautiful gardens are not made, by sighing, Oh how beautiful, and sitting in the shade."
> •

Be sure to label each plant as all look alike when still small. Many of these will be available in the marketplace in August and September. It is too early to direct sow cool season greens and radishes.

If there are young plants of tomatoes available, set out a few for a fall crop. This is a gamble, and when weather cools in fall, they will grow slower, but you may be lucky and harvest some even in late October. Corn will soon be ready and raccoons will raid the garden. They seem able to get over or under any fence. Set the Havahart trap now, using most any sweet bait, even sweet rolls. Take any captured critters — hopefully it won't be a skunk — for a long ride but don't release them near someone else's garden. Have the dog stay out overnight and hope he doesn't go to sleep.

In the flower garden, pull out any tired annuals and sow zinnias of dwarf cultivars for fall display. These are usually less troubled by mildew. Cut back petunias that are going to seed and give fertilizer for a second surge of growth. Angelonias that receive this treatment will continue to be colorful until frost. Gather flowers for drying. (See **Drying Flowers For Winter Decoration** in **Chapter 3, A Year in the Herb Garden**.) Gomphrena, strawflower and statice are thriving and removing blooms will encourage more to come. Irises and daylilies may be dug and divisions replanted. Use herbs to liven up bland foods. (See **Recipes** for herb butter and herb vinegar in **Chapter 3, A Year in the Herb Garden**.)

## ❖ AUGUST ❖

Only the heat tolerant flowers are still attractive. Early in this month as the days get shorter and the temperature falls slightly, buds begin forming on the early chrysanthemums. At 35 degrees latitude, in the Huntsville area, on August 31, days are 13 hours long. This is when the mid-season chrysanthemums, the majority of which are grown in pots for sale, begin bud formation. Artificial light from street lights or other sources that prolong the "day" will prevent buds from forming. Those in the garden have a good root system and will begin forming buds before this date. Don't worry too much if there are dead leaves on the lower stems. If watered, they bloom fairly well and the stems will not show. Nierembergia 'Purple Robe' continues to bloom on six-inch tall plants with cup-shaped, one inch up-facing blooms. Drought tolerant 'Lamb's Ears' send up bloom spikes, but the flowers are not showy and are best removed. The wooly gray foliage gives contrast with bright blooms of petunias and pentas. Perennial asters (aster x frikartii), almost shrubs, will bloom late this month and are good background plants that are not hindered by lack of water in late fall. In the foreground, annual lantana continues to spread and roots form in moist soil. The only perennial lantana, 'Miss Huff,' also spreads and attracts butterflies with its orange, yellow and pink blooms. The dwarf zinnias planted in July have begun to bloom. Keep spent blooms removed and you will have a nice display until frost. Ornamental grasses are showy at this season. Continue to gather seed heads of grasses and other materials for drying. If you plan to make a wreath using dried herbs and flowers, gather large quantities of many different things. Wild plants also provide interesting materials.

In the shade garden, drooping bell-shaped blue flowers of adenophora 'Ladybells' are blooming on two-foot stems. Roots creep into damp places, however, it is not an invasive plant. Coleus need bloom spikes removed for more colorful leaves. Fibrous rooted begonias, such as the 'Dragon Wing' with red or pink blooms are excellent for shade or sun. Caladiums send up bloom stems, but cut them off and hope the colorful leaves continue until frost cuts them down. These tender bulbs are best dug and kept in sawdust or other dry storage until late spring. Scooping out a small part of the center of a large bulb or planting it upside down (on purpose) is said to promote more leaves.

Winter squashes are nearing maturity, but do not gather any that still have green streaks. They will not keep, and flavor is not yet fully developed. Pick mature ones with a stem, which will require a sharp pruner to cut. Cure in a warm location for a week and then store in a cool location. Cut off tops and dig sweet potatoes carefully to avoid damage to the roots. (See **Sweet Potatoes** in **Chapter 6, Variety of Vegetables**.)

Water corn so the kernels will be plump when the ears mature. Remove damaged leaves from tomatoes and if the indeterminate plants are still vigorous and have outgrown their cages, cut them off above a sucker growing a few feet below the top of the cage and give fertilizer for late fruits. Fruit worms will become more prevalent and attack peppers as well as tomatoes. Look for entry holes on the tops of fruits and remove any showing this condition. Early or late each day, watch for the tomato hornworm and pick them off and kill them. Peppers will bloom again when cooler weather occurs and if excess blooms appear, thin them out. There will be fewer, but larger peppers, and more will ripen before frost. Many cucumbers are being produced and you may need to learn some new recipes to keep up with production. Insects are numerous and spraying will probably be needed to get usable fruits. Try some of the new products that are now available for organic gardeners.

As the summer vegetables are harvested, this is the beginning of that second chance. Cucumbers are about over, but there is not time to sow a late crop of these. Pull them out, and in mid-month, sow 'Roma' beans and let them climb on the same trellis. You will get some harvests before frost if water and fertilizer are applied. If the fall brassica seedlings are ready, set them out where vacant spaces allow. Deer and rabbits are waiting for you to grow these delicacies. If cutworms are a problem, use a foil collar or other protection. Collards, kale, turnips and other greens that are direct sowed may be protected by applying diatomaceous earth or finely crushed egg shells on top of the row. Be sure to thin these as needed.

Continue to harvest okra and corn, if the raccoons did not get them. Pull out the stalks and save a few good stalks for fall decoration. Keep them in a dry place until October. Those not to be saved can be chopped — a tremendous job — to add to the compost pile. Corn was a heavy feeder and whatever is planted after it, needs lots of fertilizer. All summer squash vines are drying up or disease or stem borers have killed them. Remove and destroy them and also turn under mulch that surrounded them. Dill can be sowed in any vacant places and will entice pollinators to work all crops. Any plants allowed to go to seed will provide volunteer seedlings early next spring. Field peas of any type are ready to be picked or let dry on the vines for dry use. Lima beans have the same characteristics and also are used fresh or dried.

Cut out and destroy the canes of blackberries that bore fruit. They are drying up and will die soon. This will provide needed space for the new canes that will fruit in the next year. Any roots that have emerged outside of the allotted space can be dug and potted to give away or set in vacant spaces. Tie up long canes to keep in bounds. Replant strawberry plants using the "daughter" plants that grew nearest the fruiting plants of spring. (See **Chapter 2, Small Fruits**.) Remove offsets that have formed on the ones you set out. This will keep the patch from getting too crowded and give energy to the new plants for bearing next spring. Sidedress with fertilizer at this time and keep watered.

> •
> Green mesh netting is available for row cover to protect the fall vegetables from egg-laying butterflies, rabbits and deer. It is better than the polyester cloth used as frost protection during cold months, because it allows air circulation and plants will not overheat. No spraying will be needed and your broccoli, cabbage, collards, kale and greens will be free of insect damage. When cold weather arrives, remove the mesh cover and replace it with frost protective cover.
> •

In the flower garden, keep the young zinnias watered so they will grow and bloom soon. Dahlias are blooming well. Keep dead blooms removed to encourage new ones to appear. Roses need supplemental fertilizer and disease and insect protection. If they have sent out long drooping stems, prune judiciously for a beautiful fall show. Naked ladies (Lycoris squamigera) and red spider lilies (L. radiata) will surprise you after a rain. These have remained dormant since last spring when the foliage matured and disappeared. When blooms have faded, it is time for transplanting if that is needed.

There will be large pots of mum plants for sale and they are impressive and expensive. Choose plants that are just coming into bloom for the longest display. These can be used to add color on the patio or even planted in the garden. They will require lots of water while potted and if you decide to set them in the garden, do not be disappointed if they do not survive the winter. The roots have filled the pot and need to be spread and encouraged to grow into surrounding soil to endure cold weather. This process stresses the plant and water will be needed if rain does not occur. If we have many weeks before winter arrives, the plant will have a better chance of survival. All mums benefit from having the dead tops remain through the winter, as nature intended. (Messy until March!)

## ❖ SEPTEMBER ❖

At last, we receive relief from the heat and it is comfortable to be in the garden. This is usually a dry month and water is necessary for the last flowers of summer. Hybrid cultivars of goldenrod are backgrounds for shorter perennials and the dark green foliage of rosemary makes good background for mid-height flowers. Angelonias and dahlias continue to bloom if spent flowers are removed.

Sternbergias also surprise us because they, too, were completely absent until bloom season. Leaves will join the yellow crocus-type flowers very soon and remain until frost kills them. These are plant locations that we need to identify to avoid digging and damaging them while they are dormant. Gomphrena, strawflowers and statice continue to produce flowers for drying. Gather and preserve herbs for winter. Keep gathering dried materials for the craft projects.

## In the Greenhouse

Take cuttings of outdoor tender plants that you want to grow for next year. Herbs, such as pineapple sage, lemon verbena, scented geraniums and velvet sage are marginally hardy and may or may not survive winter. Rosemary cuttings root easily at this season. All cuttings root readily before cooler weather tends to harden the tissue of stems. Use those plastic cake covers that you have saved for closed containers that provide humidity and help cuttings to root. (It is a benefit to be able to see roots as they form in these transparent containers.) If it is still too hot in the greenhouse, root them under fluorescent light. (See **Fluorescent Light Gardens** under **January** in this chapter.) Sow lettuce seeds for keeping in the greenhouse during winter. You will be glad to have 'Green Ice' and 'Red Sails' to add to salads in December, January and February.

Clean up houseplants that have been on the patio and bring them inside before the heat is turned on. This will give them a chance to become gradually adjusted to drier air.

Enjoy the bright colored blooms of fall. The colors are more intense when cool weather arrives and it is a pleasure to go to the garden and not suffer in heat. Joe Pye Weed, golden rod and other wild flowers have been hybridized and there are dwarf cultivars that fit in a garden and behave better than the wild ones. Gaillardias and black-eyed Susans will continue to bloom until hard frost. This is the time to divide the spring blooming perennials. Shasta daisies and May or oxeye daisies (Chrysanthemum leucanthemum), tall garden phlox, veronica, yarrow (achillea), perennial dianthus such as 'Bath's Pink,' and fern-leaf coreopsis all transplant best at this season.

Columbine is a short-lived perennial. Volunteer seedlings that will not necessarily be like the original plants may be moved easily if the deep root is not damaged. Sweet William seedlings may be set in new locations to bloom in spring. These will have a month or two to get well established before winter sets in. Excellent mulch for perennials and strawberries can be had by raking up fallen pine straw before the leaves of deciduous trees join them. Bag and keep dry until needed. This is the last chance to treat deciduous tree seedlings with herbicide before they go dormant. (See **Removing Unwanted Tree Seedlings** at the start of this chapter.)

If you have not planted fall vegetables, it is not too late. Greens and turnips are quick to germinate and grow fast if fertilizer and water are given. Do not delay thinning those that are crowded. Broccoli and cabbage may not mature before severe weather, but collards, kale and spinach are extremely hardy and survive and grow through most winter months. Brussels sprouts planted now will still produce those tiny cabbage heads about mid-December. Sow carrots and radishes of various kinds. Carrots sometimes do well through winter and other times they do not mature before the hot weather arrives and then are strong flavored and tough. Daikon radishes will grow through winter and provide harvests when not much else is available. Small red globe radishes will produce in a month or more and have good flavor due to cooler soil.

There will still be a few more tomatoes, peppers, eggplants and okra before the cooler weather makes them slow down or frost takes its toll. Finish harvesting winter squash, melons, field peas, limas and other beans. Gather green peppers even if they are small. They are still edible and maybe you have some large red or yellow ones that are especially flavorful. Peppers are easy to freeze. Seed, cut into usable pieces, and freeze in layers for later use. They will be too limp when thawed for raw use, but are excellent for pizza, soup and casseroles. Okra may be sliced and frozen for soups and casseroles without blanching. Place slices on a sheet of waxed paper on a tray and freeze, then bag. Turn any vacant spaces while the weather is dry. This is an excellent time to sow cool season grasses to fill any vacant places in the lawn. Over seeding Bermuda lawns with annual rye is often done, but if there will be lots of leaves to rake, this is not a good idea.

## ❖ OCTOBER ❖

Pansies and violas are plentiful and if deer and rabbits are not a problem, be sure to plant some. Try some of the new Wave types. Choose the smaller plants that are not in bloom. You want them to get established before giving all energy to flowering. Consider using hyacinth bulbs as an under planting and parsley makes a good companion plant for pansies and violas. Bulbs are plentiful in the market place. Do not leave them in a hot car while you shop or they will not survive. The most dependable are daffodils. Double or triple bulbs can be divided before planting or left as a group. (See **Daffodils** under **March** in this chapter.)

Mail order catalogues of bulbs have special offers at this time. Try something new such as 'Spring Starflower' (Ipheion). They do well in deciduous shade, bloom in late March at a height of four inches and are deer proof. Cut off peony tops and discard. Larkspur, poppy, cornflower and nigella are germinating. Thin and transplant crowded ones while still small. Separate and plant garlic cloves saved from the July harvest. Those in the grocery store are of unknown cultivars, and it is questionable if they will thrive in our climate or be free of disease. Pull out basil plants and scatter seeds for volunteer plants of unknown cultivars next spring.

Dig peanuts and leave them on the stems to dry for several weeks before separating from the vines. Roast in the shell in a single layer at 350 degrees for about 20 minutes. Do not let them burn! When it smells good, taste one. They will continue to cook after being removed from the oven.

Harvest pumpkins with a stem and use them with corn stalks and potted mums for decoration. When frost is threatened, pick green tomatoes for ripening. Wrap each one in paper and place in a single layer in a tray, but not in the sun. Turnips and greens will be ready soon if not now. A little frost will improve the flavor. If they have not grown much, give liquid fertilizer high in nitrogen.

## ❖ NOVEMBER ❖

Frost is expected at any time, but often there is a period of mild weather after the first hard freeze. If you have a wonderful display of mums, cover them with spun bonded polyester or an old sheet fastened with clothespins for a night. Gather the last bouquet of your favorite flowers. Maybe they are roses. Roses may be pruned lightly at this time to avoid storm damage in winter.

If peony roots were ordered, they will arrive this month. Prepare the planting places ahead of time and when they are delivered, immediately get them set out. If you dig a peony to share with a friend, use a strong tool (maybe a screw driver?) to remove most of the soil and then divide the root while taking care not to injure the growing tips. If some parts of the root are broken off, make a clean cut before replanting.

This is the ideal time to plant trees and shrubs as their roots will get established during the winter months. Get all bulbs planted and record all of these events in your journal. Read back on early entries and jot down results of various successes and, hopefully, no failures.

> • Peony roots are never seen in the marketplace when fall arrives. Complete dormancy, in colder climates where most are grown, does not occur in time for preparation of quantities of roots to be packaged. These duties and shipping cannot be completed before the holiday shopping season begins and possible buyers have lost interest in outdoor gardening.
> •

The gardening year is drawing to a close, but there are still chores to be accomplished before we put the garden to bed. Enjoy the fall leaves of blueberries before they are shed. Rake pine needles and bag or use now for mulch.

Deciduous trees are shedding their leaves and either chop them by mowing and leave on the lawn, or rake and give to any vegetable gardener in the neighborhood — if you do not make compost. If you have access to a shredder, shred leaves, moisten lightly and bag them. Decomposition will occur to some degree even in cold weather. Add a sprinkle of compost to hasten the process. If you turn the bag a few times, that will mix the contents to help it take place. Remove dead foliage of perennials and pull out annuals. Leave the mums "messy until March."

There are several gingko trees on the east side of the Von Braun Complex and it is interesting that these "golden gingkos" shed nearly all of their leaves in just a few days. The female of this species produces foul smelling fruits, so we are glad that all used in landscaping are male trees. (The fruits, when fresh, are eaten in the Orient.) The scion (upper part) of the tree is taken from a male tree and grafted on to a root stock (underground root) of unknown sex to guarantee that the tree will not produce fruit. Fossils have been found containing the distinctive fan-shaped leaf of this tree, so it has been in existence for millions of years. It is an amazing sight to see the grass covered with yellow leaves. This is the only known deciduous tree that behaves in this way.

## In the Greenhouse

Remove shade cloth as the days become shorter and often cloudy. If at all possible, provide warm water for greenhouse plants. The shock of cold water will slow down their growth. Recently potted cuttings need less water and very little fertilizer during the gloomy weather of winter. Dahlias that have been dug can be stored under the greenhouse bench where it is cool but protected from freezing. If they are not free of soil, put them in heavy paper bags to keep things neat. It is helpful to label the colors for planning color schemes in spring. Occasionally check on them to be sure they are not too wet or too dry. Potted amaryllis that have been kept dry for a few months may be gradually moistened and brought into bloom for the holidays. Continue to train any topiary rosemary plants and get them ready for gift giving. Sow lettuce seeds for an indoor crop to be added to winter salads when the previous crop has been harvested. The greenhouse gives much pleasure when we cannot work out of doors.

If the shorter days of this season get you down, do as Kipling advised when he wrote:

> "The cure for an ill, is not to stay still
> Or sit with a book by the fire —
> But to take a large hoe and a shovel also,
> And dig til you gently perspire."

> To this I add the following:
> "Or just go the greenhouse, that place
> To forget about the human race
> And plant and pot and relax with
> Plants in your own private space
> Where no stress is required."

Harvest your fall vegetables and plan to use them for holiday meals. Swiss chard may not survive the winter, so use it now. Add herbs to the Thanksgiving feast. The parsley sowed several months ago is ready to be used for garnishing. It also serves as a breath freshener. You can be justifiably proud if you have broccoli, cabbage, collards, kale and kohlrabi to serve. Use turnips before they get too large. The white

Oriental cultivars are especially tender and sweet. Brussels sprouts will be ready for meals later. Use sweet potatoes and winter squash. It may require some strength to cut butternut, but when baked, sprinkled with a little ginger or cinnamon and butter, you will decide gardening is a worthwhile endeavor. Check on the green tomatoes every week and discard any that have spoiled.

## ❖ DECEMBER ❖

Holidays will be here soon. Use your dried herbs and flowers to make unique gifts. I have made dried flower and herb wreaths in years past. (This requires many hours!) The recipients were much appreciative and wished I had told them to open the gift before they had parties so they could be displayed when guests arrived. Fresh greenery wreaths may be constructed of a combination of several shrubs or just one broad leaf evergreen. Berries of holly and nandina add interest. (Artificial berries last longer.) Female native cedars have blue green berries that add interest to wreaths. Small apples and pomegranates also may be used. If not displayed in the sun, they will remain attractive for a month. Cones of all sizes are interesting additions or a wreath of cones decorated with ribbon is effective. Many books on this subject are available in libraries.

In Huntsville, visit the main library and enjoy the Christmas trees trimmed in many different types of decorations, some of which are from plant societies. Take advantage of the many community festivities of the season.

### In the Greenhouse

Lettuce is ready, cuttings need potting and any plants such as rosemary will be much appreciated gifts for fellow plant enthusiasts. Poinsettias are available in all colors and sizes. Much care was taken to produce these and even if the foil wrap is attractive, either punch holes in the bottom of it and place the plant in a saucer, or remove the wrap. Keep the plant slightly moist and as warm as you would like to be. Other gift plants prefer cool temperatures and will remain attractive longer if that is provided.

Brussels sprouts may be ready to enjoy along with other fall vegetables such as collards, kale and greens. Dig clumps of chives and add to the indoor or greenhouse garden. Tomatoes may still be ripening and useable. Continue to use your winter squashes and frozen berries. Pies made from home-grown pumpkin are just too tedious. Open a can or buy one already prepared. Add all healthy garden trimmings to the compost. Be sure fences are secure to protect hungry wildlife from your garden. On mild days, look for hardy cyclamen blooms and budding early blooming shrubs. Cornelian Cherry (Cornus mas) will bloom soon, as yellow buds open. Spirea and forsythia often show a few blooms before the turn of the year. Feed the birds and provide fresh water.

As the end of the year grows near, I like to reflect on "why I garden?" Good exercise may be had while observing interesting events taking place in the world around me. I have enjoyed flowers for many decades and I see in one of my journals, written decades ago, "I have more flowers than I have ever had!" This was one of the reasons I became a flower show judge and chrysanthemum judge.

The principle reason for me to grow vegetables is that I object to eating chemically-treated fresh foods. We love the flavor of salt, sugar and fats in our food and most that are in cans, precooked or served in restaurants have these additions added to improve flavor. "You are what you eat." The convenience of having a supply at hand is important when you haven't time for searching out desired foods although organic vegetables are displayed in most stores. Most tomatoes and cucumbers are coated with "food grade paraffin" and I wash them in hot water to remove as much as possible.

Products from foreign countries are especially rejected. We have many controls on foods produced in our country, but imported ones may be treated with numerous pesticides. They surely have been treated with preservatives, to have traveled so far and still be edible. Population increases have made it important to treat the planet with kindness. After reading these suggestions on gardening in zone 7a, I hope you have gained inspiration to make your own little "heaven" of a garden and leave the world a better place than when you arrived.

**An old Chinese proverb states:**

"To be happy one day, get drunk on good grog.

To be happy one week, kill the fat hog.

To be happy one month, marry a young wife,

But make a fine garden and
<u>B</u>e <u>H</u>appy <u>F</u>or <u>L</u>ife."

*Thank you to Andria Cummings for editing my writing and keeping me focused on producing this book. Andria was recognized as "Master Gardener of the Year" in 2014 by the Master Gardeners of North Alabama and is currently a Master Gardener in Alabama and Georgia.*

•

*Thank you to Cathy Gamble (I.D. Marketing & Design, Inc.) for the book layout and design and for patience when I bogged down. Cathy is currently a Master Gardener Intern with MGNA.*

•

*Greatest appreciation to Robert McNabb, husband of 70 plus years and photographer extraodinaire, for always solving my problems when I said, "Help, this computer is not doing what I tell it to do!"*